OVERHAUL

kris gebhardt
co-written with heather lowhorn

Published by GCI Press
6407 N. Carrollton Ave.
Indianapolis, IN 46220

LCCN:

Printed in the United States of America.
10 9 8 7 6 5 4 3 2 1

Cover and interior photography by Steven Hill Photography
Layout and design by Velikan Illustration/Graphics

The author and publisher assume no responsibility for any injury that may occur as a result
of attempting to do any of the movements, techniques or exercises descibed in this book.
This book requires strenuous physical activity and a physical examination is advisable
before starting this or any other exercise program.Individual results will vary. The information
in this book is based on the author's personal experience.

Preface

I hope my story will serve as a model for self-change and the pursuit of personal excellence. Put this book on your desk or coffee table so it can be an anchor, a constant reminder of your own potential greatness.

kris gebhardt

Everybody wants to look their best, feel attractive, have endless energy to burn, and be in great shape. Nobody can deny the truth in this statement Think about it—deep down don't you harbor thoughts like, "Boy, I would like to look like the model on the magazine cover ... be that fit person on the TV commercial ... walk down the beach without reserve in a swimsuit ... be attractive and confident like the actor on my favorite TV show ...”?

If you surveyed most people you would find that the majority truly believe they deserve to feel attractive, have a fit body, be energetic and live long, healthy lives. But most are confused and disappointed because that has not been the case. Most are experiencing life as the opposite—worn out, run down, out of shape, overwhelmed, unattractive, ashamed of their overall appearance. Most people don't know that there is another option. Nor do they realize they could completely turn their lives around. They don't have to live with self-loathing. They can gain control over their body and appearance forever! I know. My name is Kris Gebhardt. I was one of

those people who secretly thought I deserved to look and feel good but figured it wasn't possible for me. I had plenty of excuses: I wasn't born with the right genes, economic status, physical characteristics or ability. But one day I decided I was through being overweight, broke and unhappy. I set out to live the life I had secretly dreamed about. It seemed a million miles away then, but today I have that life.

In my previous books; *Training Yourself, Training the Teenager for the Game of Their Life, Body Mastery and Why Weight*; I told people how to train. I told them what they should do. The information in all of those books was excellent, but when I spoke with people in interviews or during speaking engagements, no one asked me what they should do. Instead I found that people always asked me what I did. They asked how I got started, what my training schedule was, what foods I ate. I wondered why people wanted to know what I did. My life wasn't the same as theirs, and what worked for me might not work for them. But as I thought about it, their questions made sense.

Preface

In my work with some of the most successful people in the world, I too had questioned them about how they spent their time, how they had started out, what their priorities were. I didn't want them to tell me what they thought I should do, because that didn't fundamentally change me. That only addressed a specific situation. But if I could find out the principles they lived by and apply them to my life, that would change me in a lasting sense.

So my goal in writing this book is not to tell you the reader what I think you ought to do, but to tell you what I did—mistakes and all—to share the true experience that has allowed me to forever change my body and my life. My hope is that with this approach you will be better able to learn from my successes and mistakes and therefore be more successful with your own overhaul.

overhaul: A total reinventing, rebuilding, and remaking of myself. It was a discovery that not only helped me shed 60 pounds, but took me from the cellar of despair to the pinnacle of personal excellence. This philosophy has helped me gain control over my appearance, physical destiny and confidence for ever!

It is curious to me how few people are happy with their appearance. Ask anyone on the street if they are happy with their appearance and you will be amazed at the overwhelming number who say no way! And even worse, many of them readily accept that it's just the way it is. They feel it's hopeless. There is nothing they can do about it. It's out of their control, and that's the way it's supposed to be!

Well I'm here to tell you that it doesn't have to be this way...

As successful as I have been, I have to admit that for years I stumbled with the process. I failed following radical diets and marathon sessions of exercise. The simple truth is my success was not the result of stumbling onto a another exercise program or miracle diet. My success has been the result of an

Overhaul: Reinvent, Rebuild, and Remake Yourself reveals the success formula that you need to make the changes you secretly desire. I am going to share with you the program that I discovered is the key to a new you! The key to mastering your body, fitness level and appearance for good!

Preface

I feel a great author is really a good reporter. Most reporters investigate and report. In Overhaul I'm not just reporting what I have learned from investigating, I am happy to say that I am reporting what I have learned from valuable personal experience. I have lived the experience myself. You might say that I have a Ph.D. in "having done it!"

My primary objective is to convince the average person, who according to the most recent surveys is unfit, out of shape and unhappy with their appearance, that they can turn it around. They can become as attractive and fit as they desire and sport the image of their dreams regardless of their current condition, level of experience, monetary status, position in life or education. Keep this in mind as you read through the chapters of this book and see the amazing before and after pictures of my own overhaul—a transformation that took me from what my publicist calls a "fat, ugly duckling" (ouch!) to a "handsome, buff guy."

I've just turned forty and I have to tell you, this has been an interesting way to go through life. I'm in great shape; I feel good about my appearance; I have endless energy; I'm confident and ready to tackle life's challenges. It makes me wonder how so many people manage to make it any other way.

I don't have a wall full of degrees. I'm a regular guy—a college drop out, actually. Even though I didn't spend years studying exercise science or health, I was able to experience amazing success. I hope that inspires you. Don't feel as though your success will be hampered by a lack of education or experience. After reading my personal story you'll conclude that if success was possible for a guy like me, it is possible for you, too. I hope my story will serve as a model for self-change and the pursuit of personal excellence. Put this book on your desk or coffee table so it can be an anchor, a constant reminder of your own potential greatness.

Let it proudly remind you that what you are now has no bearing on what you can be.

Preface

table of contents

continued next page

table of contents continued

SNAPSHOT *from fat boy to fitness icon*

INTRODUCTION

By Heather Lowhorn

Introduction

In 1995 I was an editor for a sports publishing company when a manuscript titled "Body Mastery" landed on my desk. I liked it right away. It was different from the cut-and-dried weightlifting books I was used to seeing. So many books are written to assuage an author's ego or under the misguided belief that publishing a book will make them instantly rich. But this author seemed genuinely passionate about helping people improve their bodies and their lives. I wasn't completely sold, though. I still hadn't met the author. Would he be one of those hyperactive fitness gurus you see on TV? Or would he the stereotypical narcissistic weightlifter, always checking himself out in the mirror?

I was pleasantly surprised when Kris Gebhardt walked in. He was soft-spoken, yet confident. He was conscientious and eager to help in any way he could. I thought to myself, "What do you know, he practices what he preaches." That was the start of a wonderful business relationship that has lasted through seven years and four books. I still enjoy working with Kris.

And Kris is still genuinely passionate about helping people become the best they can be. His vision has never wavered, even when faced with obstacles that would have had most people throwing up their hands and walking away in frustration. If anything, Kris has become more focused on his goal. He is driven to get his message out.

The Eighth Wonder of the World!
Kris and Angela enjoy a reception under the dome of the historic West Baden Hotel which just underwent a $30 million renovation. The couple are consulting on the design of a world-class spa that will be included in the second phase of the renovation.

Getting the Message Out

It was early, but Kris had already been up for several hours. He was mid-way through an East Coast publicity tour promoting his book, *Training Yourself*. On this day he was appearing on a New York-area morning news show. The interview started out normally. Kris was introduced, they showed the startling photos of him overweight and out of shape at age 20 and in his current peak condition. They asked him about touring with John Mellencamp as his trainer, about training the CEO's of Fortune 500 companies, about training the cast members of the Tony- and Emmy-winning Broadway show *Blast*.

But somewhere in the questions, the interview changed. The interviewer began to lean forward, and her questions came more quickly. She was obviously intrigued by Kris' philosophy and the interview became more of a conversation.

"I wore size 40 jeans, and I had to lie down to button them. I couldn't put them in the dryer because they'd shrink, and I had to wear them all week so they would stretch enough to be comfortable. I said, 'This is enough.'" Kris explained how his life changed by making a simple decision at his kitchen table. "I sat down at the table a 250-pound person, and I stood up a fit person. All I did was change my mind."

Success!

After three previous publishing disasters, Kris' fourth book, *Training Yourself*, was a hit! Media outlets that had previously rejected his approach to fitness began to clamor for interviews. Interviewers referred to him as "the author with muscles" and opened up to his unique idea of treating fitness as a form of self-development.

On TV in the big apple
Kris, Angela and their son Kristian head out for a busy day of media interviews in the Big Apple during the book tour for *Training Yourself*. Kris found interviewers very receptive to his philosophy.

She asked what kind of education he had and was surprised by the answer. "I've never had any formal training in fitness," Kris replied. "I was this person who worked in corporate America. I didn't have time to go to a gym. I didn't have the money for a personal trainer. I had to figure this out."

"No kidding?" she asked. "You did that on your own?"

"All on my own in my own home. I've never trained in gyms," he answered.

She seemed incredulous. "You went from paunchy to buff on your own ... "

As Kris explained that he had become fit by focusing on the mental aspects of healthy living, she was obviously intrigued by Kris' philosophy.

From fat boy to photos with a supermodel.
Kris poses with Elaine Irwin Mellencamp during a photo shoot for Training Yourself. Over a thousand photos of the pair were taken in just two hours.

the segment. As the music played and the producer cut to a commercial, the interviewer continued to question Kris about the mind's role in physical training.

Interview after interview went the same way. No one asked about what exercises to do, what foods to eat. There were few questions about his famous clients. The interviews, often to the host's surprise, focused on the mental aspects of training. For Kris, this was a welcome turn-around from the media's response to *Body Mastery*.

In the mid-90s, media interviewers had tried to mold Kris into something he wasn't. "They urged me to say I had some type of health and fitness degree. I don't. I'm not that guy. I'm the college drop out. I'm the guy who had a family to support. I'm the guy who didn't have time or money to go to a gym. But I still succeeded. That should encourage people. What good are health and fitness degrees if you are so out of shape that you can't walk up a flight of stairs?"

"I saw myself as in shape, and everything I did from that point on was in support of being fit."

"It was up here first," she said, tapping her temple with her finger. "You really decided that was it, and you never looked back."

"Thought precedes action," replied Kris.

The interviewer was ready with another question when her co-anchor had to interrupt her to end

Frustrated by the media's attempt to make him into something he wasn't, Kris had sworn off publicity tours. Several years later when he published *Training Yourself*, he reluctantly agreed to interviews to promote his book. This time around, though, the media welcomed his perspective. His message hadn't changed, but people were coming around to the idea that the mind is the crucial element of fitness. No one was looking for one magic exercise that would result in the perfect body. Now people were interested in a mindset that would result in lasting change. Kris never doubted his philosophy was right, but it was a long road.

From Fat Boy to Hard Body

Kris had always struggled with being overweight. He went from a chunky child wearing husky-sized jeans to a 200-pound high school freshman. In college he topped the scales at 245. He knew the pain of being the fat kid in school. Fortunately, football offered Kris a place to fit in and introduced him to weight lifting. In football his large size was an asset, and he relished it. In college, he earned a scholarship position on the Ball State football team.

"I ate and drank everything in sight, all in the name of football. During those days, I could drink a case of beer and eat a large pizza as an after-dinner snack. Once I bet a friend that I could eat 20 White Castle hamburgers. I ate the hamburgers, burped, then ate three peanut butter and jelly sandwiches for dessert," said Kris.

During his junior year, however, a knee injury ended Kris' football dreams. With his football scholarship gone, Kris was forced to drop out of school. The same week his college football career ended, Kris' found out that he was about to become a father. His girlfriend was pregnant. Kris' life took an immediate and unexpected turn. Two weeks earlier, he had been a college football player drinking beer and eating every-

Now that's an overhaul!
Kris reinvented, rebuilt and remade himself from 250 pounds of jiggle to a 180-pound hard body. What's even more amazing is that Kris achieved this transformation on his own in his basement.

thing in sight. Now he was a college drop out with no means of supporting a new family.

Luckily, a friend found Kris a job in Michigan as a circuit court deputy, escorting prisoners from the lock-up to their court appearances. It was an hourly job with no benefits, but it was the only option Kris had. He and his girlfriend got married, moved to Michigan and rented a one-room apartment.

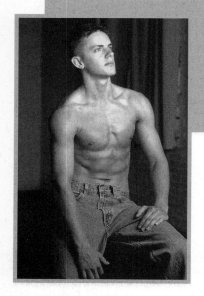

"It broke me," said Kris. "I had to ride my bike—we didn't have a car—to the store to buy my wife a $99 wedding ring." The toll on his body was high, too. Kris still had his poor eating habits, but no time to exercise. The football conditioning that had kept him somewhat muscular was a thing of the past. Add to that the stress of supporting a new family, and Kris gained even more weight. He was now up to 250 pounds.

The job wasn't a sure-thing, though. In order to keep his job as a deputy, he had to attend the police academy. And in order to attend the academy, he had to pass several tests—a complete background investigation, academic and psychiatric tests, physical exams and a series of physical fitness tests. Everything looked good except the physical exams and the fitness tests. Kris realized that he might not be accepted into the police academy because of his physical condition. He had to face the horrible fact that he might be unable to support his family because he was overweight and out of shape.

His back against the wall, Kris knew he had to change. He sat down at the table in his family's one-room apartment and made a decision. He decided enough was enough. He was going to reshape his body. On that day he began to see himself as someone who succeeded in life. He dug in and started to eat better and exercise. Two months later and 30 pounds lighter, he passed the exam and was accepted into the 37th Mid-Michigan Police Academy. "During my police training, I learned to value life," said Kris. "For 17 weeks of training, nearly everything I experienced related to life and death situations. I learned that no one is invincible and how delicate life really is. We can be here today and gone tomorrow. And I began to realize just how important our bodies are."

The Immeasurable Value of Health

While his job paid the bills and his body was improving, Kris knew his life was no success. Fortunately, a new opportunity opened up for him. The same friend who had helped Kris get hired as a deputy told him about a job working for Domino's Pizza. The founder and then-president of Domino's, Tom Monaghan, needed someone to start a security detail for him. Kris knew this was an amazing opportunity, he just didn't realize how working for Monaghan would dramatically change his life.

Kris took the job. As part of his training, he attended a school run by former Secret Service members. This training only reinforced what Kris had learned during his time at the police academy, but with a new twist. "I began to realize that, though people are killed by guns and violence every day, more people die because of poor health," he said. "They drag themselves through a kind of slow suicide by ignoring proper nutrition and the right kind of exercise."

Kris was beginning to realize the driving purpose of his life. But it took a freezing, snowy Michigan morning to crystallize his vision. Part of Kris' job doing security for Tom Monaghan included running six miles with him every morning. But certainly not this morning, thought Kris. It was 5:30 a.m. The temperature was -5 with a wind chill of -20. It was hard just to walk from the car to Monaghan's door, let alone jog for an hour. Kris thought they would bag the jog, and he could catch a nap. But Monaghan came out in his running clothes, seemingly unaffected by the cold. "Good morning," he said. "Let's run."

That was a defining moment in Kris' life. Everything stood still. Kris thought, "This man has everything. He owns a successful business, homes, cars, jets. He has every material possession and money in the bank to spare. Yet, he gets up and runs six miles to work every morning. Why?"

On tour with a music legend

Kris and Angela arrive backstage in Frankfort, Germany, while on tour with rock star John Mellencamp. Kris toured with Mellencamp from 1997 to 2000, and the pair still get together for workouts today.

The world's most beautiful gym

Kris designed this gorgeous facility nestled into a hillside on Necker Island, a private paradise owned by Virgin Records owner Richard Bronson. The island rents for a whopping $30,000 a day.

Later Kris asked him that very question. Monaghan's answer was profound in its simplicity: "I can't do anything without my health."

The truth of Monaghan's observation stuck with Kris. He became more serious about training with an old set of weights in his home. He began to devour self-improvement books. Kris became more and more passionate about becoming the best he could be.

Soon Monaghan noticed the changes the weight training produced in Kris' body, and Kris began to train him. In the early 80s personal trainers were unheard of, but that was what Kris had become. He traveled around the world with Monaghan as his chief of security and trained him.

It was a job with wonderful perks: private jets, five star hotels, $1000 suits, company cars, and an impressive salary. But it was also a round-the-clock commitment with high stress, and Kris had a dream of owning his own business. After four years of being Monaghan's right-hand man, Kris was ready to step out on his own.

Riding the Rollercoaster of Risk

Upon his departure, Kris was given the chance to realize his dream of owning a business. A Domino's franchise was offered to him. The franchise was in his hometown of New Albany, Ind., with the option to buy other nearby stores. Kris went through the franchise training and everything was set. All he had left to do was sign the papers. He worked in the store New Year's Eve and was to sign the papers the next day. But Kris felt a gnawing in his gut. "Domino's can be a healthy product," he said, "but I was watching people abuse it. Selling triple-decker meat and cheese pizzas to terminally overweight people went against what I stood for." He left the store after midnight and told himself, "I can't do this."

It beats living out of a car

After losing the family's dream house on a business deal that went sour, Kris and Angela turned misfortune around. They recently moved into their new custom built home set on a golf course. When Kris first set out to help others find fitness, he was living out of his car. He finds this more to his liking.

It was a huge risk for Kris. He was walking away from financial security with no other means of support in sight. He wanted to own a business, but this wasn't the business for him. Instead, Kris followed his dream.

In doing so, however, Kris found himself again at rock bottom. His marriage had come apart, and he was going through a divorce. With no more company cars or clothing allowance, Kris threw everything he owned into a milk crate, bought a used car and struck out on his own to pursue a career in fitness, even though he had no formal fitness training.

In order to be close to his son, Kris settled in Indianapolis. He knew no one, and he had no job. "If I would have had anything to repossess, I would have declared bankruptcy," he said. Yet he still lifted weights and held on to his dream. It was by chance that he walked into a local fitness store looking for equipment for an acquaintance who had heard of Kris' expertise.

Kris began to talk with the owner of the store who was impressed with Kris' knowledge of weight training and fitness. Undeterred by Kris' lack of experience, the owner offered Kris a sales job on the spot.

Kris' passion for fitness quickly made him a very successful equipment salesman. In no time he was doing over a million in sales, earning a six-figure income and designing fitness facilities for universities, businesses and professional athletes.

Kris recognized by a U.S. senator

September 14, 2001, Kris was scheduled to receive an award from Senator Richard Lugar. News anchor Howard Caldwell filled in for Lugar who was rushed to Washington for an emergency session with President Bush. "It was impossible to focus on individual achievement with so much tragedy facing the nation," said Kris.

But despite all his success, Kris was still frustrated. He sold with passion, and he wanted people to find the fitness success that he had, but after the sale he found people didn't stick with it. "The commission didn't mean as much as that person succeeding," he said.

His clients mistakenly believed, as many do, that buying equipment was the answer to their fitness problems. Kris knew the answer came from within, not from any gadget, so he decided to write a book.

He worked seven days a week at the store, then came home and wrote from 11 p.m. to 3 a.m. Any author will tell you that writing a book is hard, lonely work. Add in a full-time job and most will tell you to forget it. But Kris had another issue. He is dyslexic. "I worked forever just to get 100 pages," he said. Despite those obstacles, Kris finished his first book, *Why Weight*. He paid to self-publish the book and gave it away free to his customers, hoping it would help them fit exercise and health into their lives.

One of the Midwest's premiere salons

Over 22 years ago Angela was working two jobs to put herself through beauty school. Today she owns Angela Salons, formerly Envy Design. Her talent is so in demand that some clients come from out of state and others book appointments a year in advance to secure a spot.

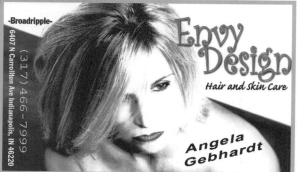

Word of Kris' hands-on experience and hard-earned knowledge began to spread. People began to come to the store, not to buy equipment, but to simply to talk to Kris and pick his brain. Not only had Kris' career taken off, but he had gotten his personal life together, too.

He had remarried a lovely woman named Angela. Angela worked in a salon and several of her customers began to tell her that people were talking to Kris for his fitness knowledge, but buying the equipment he recommended somewhere else. This only added to his frustration.

The Business Grows ... But Costs Kris his House

Kris decided it was time to concentrate on getting his fitness message out. For the second time, Kris walked away from a successful career and a handsome salary to pursue his dream. He took on a few clients to train and began to write his second book, *Body Mastery*. He and Angela also opened their own salon the week he quit his job. They went from high, steady incomes to starting two businesses. During this time Angela became pregnant, and while happy to see their family grow, self-employment left them without health insurance. Times were tight, to say the least.

Are they wearing the same swimsuit?
After giving a training seminar, Kris and Angela ham it up on the same beach where the 1999 *Sports Illustrated swimsuit issue* was shot, Virgin Gorda, British Virgin Islands.

Kris finished his manuscript and illustrated it with hundreds of photos, but he had no money to publish it as he had *Why Weight*. Undaunted, Kris used a small copier to print out 50 copies of his book. A friend in the NFL told Kris about a sports publisher he had worked with in the past. With nothing to lose, Kris sent the publisher a copy. The managing editor called him the next day. They wanted his book. Being a novice in the publishing industry cost Kris, though. Unaware of what to negotiate for, Kris made no money off the sales of *Body Mastery*. In fact, he lost money on the cost of the photography.

His business, though, was slowly growing. People were writing Kris to tell him how *Body Mastery* had improved their lives. He knew he was on the right track. His reputation was also catching the attention of some important people. Kris began training the legendary musician John Mellencamp and his wife, supermodel Elaine Erwin.

After Mellencamp's heart attack, he had begun to exercise. After discovering the benefits exercise was having not only on his health, but on his whole life, he wanted to incorporate exercise into life on the road during his concert tours. Kris traveled with Mellencamp and his band touring the country. Angela's salon was as big a success as Kris' training business. They had gambled on their dreams and were once again riding the wave of success.

Encouraged by his success, Kris still felt the best way to get his message of life-changing fitness out to people was through writing books. Working with the publishing industry was still a struggle, though. Through his publisher, Kris met a sales rep who was about to start his own publishing business. He was impressed with *Body Mastery* and wanted Kris' future books in his venture.

Kris agreed to pay the production costs while this partner paid for the printing and distribution. As with many who look for the best in themselves, Kris looks for the best in others. He saw his partner's positive qualities, but overlooked the negative ones. It was a costly mistake. After much time, effort and cost, Kris' third book, *Training the Teenager* was ready to be shipped to stores. But his relationship with his business partner had crumbled, and Kris was stunned to find himself left with a few thousand books and a bad reputation with the industry's major buyers—they were refusing to buy his books.

Rebuilding the billion dollar man
At the persuasion of John Mellencamp and Phyllis McCullough, businessman Bill Cook began training with Kris. The billionaire has gone from a gravely ill heart patient to a man with the energy of someone half his age.

During this time he and Angela had built their dream house. It was a much-deserved reward for all their hard work building their businesses. With so much money invested in producing *Training the Teenager*, the difficulties with the buyers hit at the wrong time. They were unable to close on the house. They lost the house. "It was humiliating," said Kris. "but I knew I could overcome it. I knew I could make it work."

ANGELA'S Hair Nutrients Line
Kris and Angela in a magazine advertisement for Angela's Hair Nutrients Line. Combining expertise and experience, they developed thirty hair, skin and scalp products nutritionally formulated to get your hair, skin and scalp into healthy shape.

When Beauty Meets Fitness...

Hair Care Products So Nutritious...
You Could Eat Them!

Available at -- Envy Design -- 466-7999 -- In Broadripple

Kris had seen hard times before, and he wasn't about to be beaten by this setback. Instead he got in his car and drove across the country to meet with the industry's biggest buyers in an effort to salvage his reputation. Sometimes he had to wait for hours before anyone would meet with him, once he even had to schmooze a buyer backstage during a Mellencamp concert in New York City, but his persistence paid off. After explaining the situation with his former business partner, the buyers relented. Orders for the book began to trickle in, and Kris had learned a hard lesson about choosing business associates more wisely. He had managed to salvage his reputation in the publishing industry, but the problems cost his family their dream home.

Long-Awaited Publishing Success

Always optimistic, Kris shook off the loss and never looked back. And despite the slow book orders, he was still dedicated to getting his message to people. In fact, he began to realize that people where hungry for that message. He still received letters and emails from people who had read his books thanking him for the impact on their lives. At Book Expo America in Chicago, the publishing industry's most important convention, Kris was scheduled to sign copies of *Training the Teenager*. When he arrived, he was disheartened to find himself next to two players from the Chicago Bears who were also signing books.

"I said to Angela, 'Those guys are local heroes. Everybody is going to go to their table. You better get set for two long, boring hours,'" said Kris. "What happened in the next 30 minutes completely shocked me. I signed books for a nonstop line of people. I was forced to stop signing because I ran out of books! People kept asking me if the principles in the book would work for adults. They really wanted the information."

A royal workout
Kris gets in a jog between the training seminars he gave at Drumuland Castle in Ireland.

So Kris sat down to write his fourth book, *Training Yourself*. "It was hard. In terms of my books, I had lost every fight up until that point. It was very difficult to create. It's hard to keep writing when you're losing." And he didn't have to write that book. His fitness business was unbelievably successful. He was still touring with Mellancamp, training him and his wife. He had also started to train Bill Cook, the founder and owner of the Fortune 500 company Cook Group Inc., along with several other executives from the firm. Cook Inc. had hired him to design a state-of-the-art training facility for its employees. Things were going well, but Kris' passion had not changed. He wanted everyone to know how physical fitness could improve every aspect of one's life. He also knew that many people

where in the same situation he had been in not so many years ago: struggling to just get by with no time for the gym and certainly no money for a trainer or expensive equipment. So despite three previous failures, Kris wrote *Training Yourself*.

This time people were ready for his message. Kris was amazed by the response he received to his book. People were ready to believe that the key to fitness began in the mind. Media interview after media interview, the questions focused on the mental aspects of physical fitness instead of what exercises produced "instant" results.

Kris Sees Lifesaving Results with Heart Patients

When Kris first went on tour with John Mellencamp, he was introduced to Mellencamp's cousin, Tracy Cowles. Tracy was 50, and he had had three heart attacks. "When we were introduced, he couldn't stand. He had to lean against the wall." The long-term prognosis for Cowles was not good and his health prevented him from working. He was even being prepared to be placed on the heart transplant list. Mellencamp had invited him to come on tour, too, so that he would eat right and have access to Kris. The thought was that otherwise, he would simply sit at home and die.

When Kris first began to work with him, he was afraid he was in over his head. He had never worked with heart patients before. "He does 20 pounds on the weight machine, and we have to wait 20 minutes for his heart rate to come down," he said. By working slowly with Cowles and carefully monitoring his work-outs, Cowles' life began to vastly improve. "He went from disabled to building his boat house and deer hunting. After two years, the same doctors who expected him to be dead were amazed by his improvement." Because Kris had to work so closely with Cowles, the two built a solid friendship, and Kris was pleased to have helped Cowles regain a more normal life. Kris learned a lot from Cowles, too, especially about working with clients who suffer from heart disease.

Fit for Disney!
Kris coaches cast members of Shockwave while they rehearse for a North American tour of exclusive Disney World shows.

Two years later, another heart patient came to Kris for help. Bill Cook knew Mellencamp and the way Kris had helped Cowles. Cook had spent years building his hugely successful company and becoming a billionaire, but his health was in poor shape. He was 70, and like Cowles, he had lived through three heart attacks. His circulation was poor and he was actually in danger of having his legs amputated. His doctors had told him to get his affairs in order; he wasn't expected to live long.

Even though Kris had great success with Cowles, he was still reluctant to take on another heart patient. He wasn't a doctor or physical therapist. He wasn't even a college graduate. And Cook was, after all, a billionaire with lots of lawyers. What if something went wrong? Kris had all but decided that training Cook wasn't worth the risk when he met him. "He was leaning against a wall in the same posture Tracy had been when I met him. I knew I needed to help him," said Kris.

And he has helped. Bill began to turn his health around. Soon the feeling was returning to his feet. He was feeling more energetic. He went from leg pressing 20 pounds to pressing 300

pounds. "I'm much healthier and stronger, and I feel much better," Cook said in a recent interview. "But the biggest improvement has been my endurance. Now I can go all day."

The Death of a Friend

Unlike many personal trainers, Kris doesn't intend to stay with healthy clients forever. What gives Kris a thrill is teaching someone how to take control of their body. "I want to teach them how to train themselves and move on. It's about equipping people, not maintaining them." The one exception to this rule is clients with serious health conditions. It was a hard-learned lesson.

After three years, the time had come for Kris to leave John and Elaine Mellencamp. It was a tough decision, but Kris knew it was the right one. This also meant saying goodbye to his friend Tracy Cowles. A new trainer would tour with the Mellencamps to train the band and to work with Cowles.

"I thought Tracy was still training, but eight months later, I called him and he wasn't. He was walking and things like that, but not seriously training. I told him that wouldn't cut it, and that we needed to get together." Tracy agreed but said he had hunting plans, and that they needed to meet after deer season. They never did. Cowles suffered a heart attack and died while hunting.

Cowles' death hit Kris hard. He couldn't help feeling upset. "I knew what I had done with him had worked. He went from being unable to stand to hunting and working around the house. But he had to continue with serious training. It was a very difficult funeral to attend."

A Broadway Triumph

Kris has no intention of attending a similar funeral anytime soon. He realizes that Bill Cook is someone who will probably always be a client because of his heart problems. And since Cook has been training, he shows no signs of slowing down. In fact, he has even become a producer for a Broadway show. And not just any show, but the Emmy-and Tony-winning Blast.

Blast is a high-energy show that combines physical feats with great music. Cook knew the show would be physically taxing for the performers, and he also knew that Kris' techniques for achieving peak performance were a natural fit. Kris was hired to work with the cast. In an interview for *Backstage*, Kris said, "I came on board to help them stay fit, especially when traveling, whether it's food, hydration, whatever.

Opening night!
Kris and Angela celebrate backstage at a party for the Emmy -and Tony-award-winning hit Blast! Kris trained the cast, preparing them to look their best on stage and helping them to be physically up to the rigors of nightly performances.

I put them in a training facility to teach them how to maintain themselves. The point is, no matter how exhausted they are, they can stay fit and healthy—in their bodies and in their minds." Kris has helped the performers endure the grueling schedule and look their best on stage.

Writing is a business

Kris is selected for the *Indianapolis Business Journal's* 40 Under 40. Kris is the first author to be chosen for the award. "This award is significant because it recognizes that authors are legitimate business people and validates producing books as a legitimate business venture," says Kris.

Why Not You?

The point of giving you all of this background on Kris is this: If he can do it, so can you. Anyone can. If Kris had the power to change his body from a flabby liability to a chiseled sculpture, so do you. If he could rise from financial ruin to live his dreams, so can you. He didn't have excess time or money. He didn't have powerful personal connections. He didn't have prestigious degrees hanging on his wall. But he knew what he wanted to become, and he risked everything to achieve that dream.

Kris laughs when he describes himself as a redneck from southern Indiana. "Who knew that I would travel around the world? Who knew I would meet the famous people I've met? Who knew I would be a guest on private islands and be welcomed backstage at famous venues? I was a hillbilly!"

Hillbilly or not, somewhere along the way, Kris stumbled on to the secret that what ever you have the power to dream, you have the power to achieve. That's what this book is all about. What is your dream? What do you want to achieve? Kris' hope is that in this book you will find the tools to change the way you think about yourself and your life. Fitness isn't a quick fix. It's a mindset that Kris is passionate about sharing with others. In fact, Kris and Angela have used their own resources and risked their own security trying to help others live the best life they can. Now Kris has written this book to show you the formula that will enable you to reinvent, rebuild and remake yourself. His personal success is motivating and inspiring. His unique approach to self-improvement from the inside out can improve your body, your look and your life. This book could be the first step toward realizing your dreams. Enjoy the journey.

IN MEMORY OF
Tracy D. Cowles
1947-2000

When I met Tracy he was leaning up against the wall outside the backstage dressing room door of his cousin, John Mellencamp. This former marine had once had the reputation as a bar-clearing tough guy—Jeremiah Johnson and the Marlboro Man rolled into one.

The day he stood before me, however, he was a mere shadow of that man he had been. On that day he leaned against the wall because he could barely stand. He was a man who feared every breath could be his last. He feared falling asleep because he knew he might not wake back up. In fact, he told me he had slept very little in the last two weeks because when he laid down he choked on his own blood. His doctors offered very little hope—he could die in six months or six days. He needed a heart transplant, but he was too weak for the surgery. Their outlook was very grim.

When we shook hands his grip was weak and shaky. I could see the fear in his eyes, and I sensed how defeated he felt. John had encouraged Tracy to go on tour with him and work out with me. The thought was that otherwise Tracy would simply sit around and die. Hospital bills and the hardship of being too sick to work had financially devastated Tracy. He had no means to pay me for working with him, but business didn't matter. I knew I had to help him.

For three years I pushed him in the gym. Each of us drove an hour and a half each way to meet at John's house and work out in his gym. By working together one day at a time, we battled off the grim reaper. Tracy rebuilt himself and astonished his doctors, who concluded that this man who should have been dead by now no longer needed a heart transplant. Tracy began to enjoy a more active live. He went back to deer hunting and building projects around his house.

I trained Tracy for three years. Then one night at a concert in Raleigh, North Carolina, I stood in the wings watching John rock the house. I remember it like it was yesterday. On the opposite side of the stage I saw Tracy. It was as if I was looking at him for the first time—he was that Jeremiah-Johnson-Marlboro-Man-bouncer-type again. Glancing over at John as he performed like a lean, mean rocking machine, I realized my job was done. It was time for me to move on and teach others how fitness could change their lives.

Eight months later I got the call. Tracy had walked into the woods and never come back. At his funeral Tracy's wife hugged me and thanked me for what I had done for Tracy. She told me that Tracy was able to live again and enjoy the best three years of his life because of my help. I looked her in the eye and said, "I should be thanking you. His friendship was more than money could buy."

I dedicate this h're book to my good ol' hillbilly friend. You never did whoop my ass in arm wraslin', did ya!

When you settle
for what you are
instead of what you
can be, you live in a
constant state of anxiety,
because what you are is
not what you want to be!

Reinvent

1

PART 1

Everybody wants to look their best, feel attractive, have endless energy to burn, and be in great shape. Nobody can deny the truth in this statement. Think about it...

chapter 1
become your dream

What attracted you to this book? What in your life do you want to change so badly that you reached out and picked up this book instead of all the others? Did you chose this book because you want to change your physical appearance? Think about these questions: Are you the person you want to be? Are you living the life you wish you could? Do you always look and feel your best? Do you always perform at your peak?

If not, why? What's holding you back? Your weight? Your appearance? Your lack of confidence? Be honest with yourself.

How many times has getting dressed in the morning set a bad tone for the rest of the day? Do you feel as though you're always run down, outdated, and two steps behind? Are you too humiliated to wear a swimsuit in public? Do you insist your spouse turn the light out before sex, and even then keep on as much clothing as possible? Did you catch a glimpse of yourself in the mirror and ask, "What has happened to me? Who is that stranger staring back at me?"

Maybe you've sacrificed and dedicated yourself to raising your children. Perhaps you've worked tirelessly to build a successful career. But now you find that your energy has slipped away and that you are a far cry from being motivated and inspired. You're feeling that life has taken a toll, and it shows.

Think about these questions:
Are you the person you want to be?
Are you living the life you wish you could?
Do you always look and feel your best?
Do you always perform at your peak?

I understand. I was once where you are now. I know what it is like to be unsatisfied with life. I had no money, my family lived paycheck to paycheck, I was overweight, I didn't see a future for myself. Deep down I suspected that I was worth something, but I didn't have the confidence to believe it. I felt looked-over, left behind and not worth much. When I entered a room of strangers, I felt self-conscious and awkward. I was pretty sure that I was an average guy, destined to settle down, add 10 pounds every five years and punch a time clock for the rest of my life. But when I came to that crossroads in my life, I decided to choose better for myself. I decided to believe I was important, that I could have a better life, that I could dream big and achieve those dreams. I decided to overhaul my life.

Today I barely recognize the person I was then. After my overhaul, not only did my body change for the better, but so did my entire life. I have a beautiful wife and four wonderful kids. I own two successful business, I've authored five books, I travel the world, I consult celebrities and billionaires. I live a life beyond what I could have dreamed of back then. Take my word for it: *Overhaul* changed my life; it will change yours.

Overhaul was born from my personal experience. I was tired of going on diets. I was tired of exercise programs that produced little or no results. I desired to get fit and healthy, so I set up a system that I could easily maintain for the rest of my life. I made a commitment to solve this mysterious puzzle that so many struggle with. *Overhaul* is more than a New Year's resolution,

Success is waking up today better than you were yesterday.

more than a gym membership, more than the latest diet or newest exercise apparatus. What I am going to share with you in this book are the keys I discovered to turning my life around—the keys I used to completely rebuild my body, remake my appearance, reinvent myself and transform into a confident, healthy, successful person.

> When we limit ourselves based on past experience, we short change our potential.

In *Overhaul*, I want to show you how to unleash this superstar. Uncover your own outstanding qualities and let them shine! It's time to take control of your life. Change who you are into who you want to be. You must be unsatisfied with some aspects of your life, or you wouldn't have been attracted to this book.

It's Your Choice

Let me just lay it out there for you: You are living the life you have chosen. You have the job you chose to have. You have the body you chose to have. You have the face that you chose to have. If you are unhappy and unsatisfied, you are that way because you chose it. I hope that wasn't too blunt for you, but it's the truth. Sure, life deals everyone different cards, but how you play the cards you're dealt is entirely up to you.

We justify our situations: They have personal trainers and cooks and great genes. Her parents are rich and powerful. He has an Ivy League education. I wouldn't want to be rich; too much money is corrupting. Bull. Those are just things we tell ourselves to avoid the reality that if we really wanted to be, we could be those people. Who wouldn't rather have too much money rather than too little? And that gorgeous actress may have a personal trainer now, but at one time she was probably an overworked waitress fitting in auditions on her dinner breaks. Sure, some successful people started out higher on the ladder than most, but the majority of successful people are success-ful because they took risks and worked hard and didn't give in to discouraging setbacks. They saw themselves as winners, they never wavered from that vision of themselves, and eventually the rest of the world joined them in that vision.

I'm not greedy, and I know that beauty and money don't equal happiness. That's not what I'm trying to say. There are plenty of rich, attractive, miserable people out there. It's not that if you live in the biggest house of anyone you know then you'll be happy. What you're after is the feeling of being happy with who you are. It feels great to be comfortable in your own skin. It feels great to know that you would rather have your life than anyone else's. That feeling of self-confidence comes from realizing that you are important. You are just as valuable as any politician, actor or business mogul. When you realize that you are a star, you treat yourself like one. When you treat yourself like one, others will, too.

I think attractiveness is a melting pot of confidence, worth, esteem, respect, attitude, personal style, grooming, fitness. When you blend these ingredients together, you get self-image, and your self-image defines your level of attractiveness.

Appearance Does Matter

Let's face it. Attractive people stand out. Society tends to smile on people who look good. Having experienced life from both sides of the mirror, I am uniquely aware of this truth. When I was over-weight I didn't care about my appearance or my clothes. I didn't think I was worth any extra attention, so no one else did, either. People didn't respect me, and I was easily pushed around. Looking back, I see now that I lived under a dark cloud.

After my overhaul, people treated me differently. There were more opportunities, more open doors. People seemed more eager to listen to what I had to say. Good people and good situations were attracted to me. Was this change in the world's perception of me strictly based on looks or was it because I was more confident? Probably a combination of both, but either way, I know that no matter what people say, appearance does matter. It matters a lot.

Having an attractive body and paying attention to my looks has had a huge impact on my career as an author. Writing is an isolating job, and perhaps due to being alone so much, many

> What I represent is self change, the pursuit of personal excellence. I want the changes I made in my life to inspire others to give themselves permission to become the person they truly want to be, to reach a point where they live without regret and enjoy who they are.

28

writers neglect their appearance. When it comes time to promote your book, it doesn't pay to look like death warmed over. There are thousands upon thousands of new books published each year, each with an author vying for publicity. Attractiveness gives me an added edge in snagging that publicity. The media always asks for pictures before they book you on TV and print material. I want my appearance to stand out so they will be more likely to book me for an interview instead of someone who looks as though they spend all their time in front of a computer in their basement. I can't tell you how many times my publicist has called me and told me they booked me not only because they were interested in my book, but because I looked good. Is that vain or egotistical? I don't think so. I think it's smart. I know that looking the best I can helps my career.

Set your standards high then viciously pursue them.

That brings up an important question: Just how important is your appearance? Well, experts tell us that only around 7% of communication actually comes from what we say. The largest part of how we communicate is generated by our body—eye contact, mannerisms, movement, appearance. Unfair or not, people do judge books by their covers. Whether consciously or unconsciously, people are constantly sizing you up and you are doing the same to others. Is it any wonder that fashion, beauty and fitness are all billion-dollar industries?

I'm not trying to talk you into a narcissistic obsession with your looks. I'm just letting you in on a fact of life. Looks matter. I've been a 20-year-old ugly duckling and a 40-year-old buff guy. I'd choose 40 and fit any day. Looks shouldn't consume your life, but spend a little effort on yours and you'll reap rewards.

Just What is Attractive?

A definition for attractiveness is elusive. Putting into words what makes a person attractive is hard to do, but it's never hard to recognize an attractive person. They shine. You just recognize it when you see it. I wish I could offer a concrete formula for or scientific explanation of attractiveness, but it doesn't work that way. Attractiveness isn't defined by winning a beauty contest or being crowned prom king. A "beautiful" person with a rotten attitude is unattractive right away.

Complacency should be against the law.

I think attractiveness is a melting pot of confidence, worth, esteem, respect, attitude, personal style, grooming, fitness. When you blend these ingredients together you get self-image, and your self-image defines your level of attractiveness. It's part of your identity, not just an attempt to copy magazine images. Your self-image—your attractiveness—is as unique as the lines on your fingers.

Attractiveness all comes back to being the best you can be. It's about seeing yourself as worth the effort. Take the time to care for your body, your hair, your skin. Wake up and realize what an amazing person you are. Realize that you are worth the extra effort. The second that you realize you are a glorious creation and that you will live the life you were created to live, your attractiveness skyrockets. And the way you begin to live your life from that point on will only increase that attractiveness.

Three areas of focus

I believe that there are three areas of your life that you need to focus on to dramatically enhance your appearance: self-image, physical fitness and what I call polish. These are the three areas *Overhaul* covers.

First you will learn how to reinvent yourself—wipe the slate clean and start over. You will discover how to use your mind to formulate a blue print of the person you truly wish to be. The mental stuff is first in this book for a reason. In the past I have often hesitated to discuss the mental side of physical training. I suppose I did this out of a sense of fear that people would think I was crazy, but I can say without hesitation that over 80% of the dramatic physical change in my body was mental. People scoff when I tell them that I sat down a 250-pound broke loser, and stood up a fit, successful man. All that had changed was my mind, but it was the most important change. The key to lasting physical, tangible change is in your thoughts. The mind is the architect of your body—and your life!

The secret to being in great shape has more to do with "peak performance" than calories and exercise.

Changing your self-image is the most important step you can take to transform your life. I will delve more deeply into it in the next couple of chapters. Hang on, it's groundbreaking stuff.

I like to say that the hidden gem in the book is that it teaches you how to cultivate the power within to take charge and make the positive changes that will enhance your entire being.

In the second part you will learn my amazing three-phase body rebuilding program that will get you into the best shape of your life. Getting into great shape will dramatically change your appearance. Being strong and healthy is sexy. In this section of the book, I will take you step by step through the exact program I used to completely transform and reshape my body. It's the same program I have taught to rockstars, supermodels and Broadway performers. Don't worry, it's common sense and it can fit into your lifestyle. I don't expect anyone to train eight hours a day. But a little time combined with smart training methods will give you the body that you want to take you through life.

The third section of the book is about focusing on the details, the many small touches that add up to a big impact on your attractiveness. My wife, Angela, and I have been in the salon business for 20 years, and we know the importance of the right hair, skin care, makeup and clothes—the value of personal style. Imagine how lucky I was—after I lose 60 pounds and get myself into fantastic shape, I meet and marry a real beauty who is also a style makeover expert! She worked her magic on my hair, put me on some amazing skin care products and the next thing I know I'm being recruited by a modeling agency for print and television ads! Talk about a successful makeover!

Angela will share her valuable expertise on hair and skin care, and she'll explain how the right cut, color and makeup can add to your personal style. We'll also introduce something we developed about a year ago: Angela Hair Nutrients Line. It's like a fitness program for hair and skin!

And a step beyond that is our experience with cosmetic surgery. We've seen every type from nose jobs and boob jobs to face lifts, tummy tucks and hair plugs. Clients often come to us for discrete advice on cosmetic surgery, and we've referred many of them to plastic surgeons. Sometimes cosmetic surgery is a controversial subject, but we'll give you the real scoop from people who've been there. We'll tell you what they expected and how those expectations matched up with what they got.

> **Changing your self-image is the most important step you can take to transform your life.**

Conclusion

There is a lot of great stuff in this book that will do wonders for your appearance, but I want to remind you that *Overhaul* isn't just about looks. I like to say that the hidden gem in the book is that it teaches you how to cultivate the power within to take charge and make the positive changes that will enhance your entire being.

People try to label me (and they will try to label you, too). They try to peg me as a "personal trainer," a "fitness guru," etc. That's not me. If I am an icon for anything, it's not Mr. Fitness. My goal has never been to stuff exercise down people's throats. My job is to lead by example and help others help themselves. What I represent is self change, the pursuit of personal excellence. I want the changes I made in my life to inspire others to give themselves permission to become the person they truly want to be, to reach a point where they live without regret and enjoy who they are.

33

new look. Please create a new style for me—give me a new "do!" Then one of our hairdressers will artistically create a new style that totally updates and improves their appearance. The person will see their new style, shed a few tears of joy, and hug the hairdresser, thanking her for saving their life. The person leaves feeling great about themselves. Everyone's happy, but ... A couple of days later we'll see that person out in a restaurant or at the mall, and they will have their hair styled the old outdated way. When asked why they just say, " I don't know. It just didn't feel right." And they go back to their old unhappy way.

Purely by accident I came up with this formula: see it, say it, feel it, become it!

Even though getting into shape or getting an updated look makes one look and feel much better, many still slip back into the old habits they were unhappy with. Why?

I didn't want to be one of those casualties, so I decided to figure this thing out. How was I going to be successful? How was I going to avoid slipping back to my old self?

The more I thought about this, the more I realized that I needed to get my mind in shape. I realized that our thoughts govern all our actions. These thoughts shape who we are and what we do. It became clear to me that if I wanted to be something different then what I was, I had to change my thoughts. But could it be that simple? Not exactly.

I tried changing my thoughts. I told myself I wasn't going to eat ice cream after dinner every night, only to find myself eating ice cream after dinner every night! I told myself I was going to get up early and go to the gym, and then I slept in.

Although I was positive and believed in positive thinking, simply changing my thoughts from "I'm overweight" to "I'm fit and energetic" didn't get the job done either. There had to be more to it. I wanted to be a super in-shape, handsome, fit, successful guy, but when I looked in the mirror, a 250-pound, overweight, out-of-shape, washed-up jock stared back at me. "How can I get that guy out of here?" I wondered.

One day I woke up with a crazy idea. It was actually Hollywood that inspired the idea. I remember watching a special featuring some actors, and one actor said he went so deep into a character that he actually felt like he became that person.

I thought to myself, "Man, that's the answer."

Create an "Ultimate You"

So I played Hollywood. I created a character for a movie, and I called this character the "ultimate me."

I thought about the "ultimate me" that I wanted to become. I took my time and thought deeply about it. What kind of shape would he be in? What would his body look like? What were the characteristics of his appearance? Was he well-groomed and nicely dressed? Was he confident, poised, charismatic?

I was like an actor studying a character that he was playing in a movie. I pinpointed all the traits of the character, everything I imagined would make him tick. Only I wasn't studying for a movie –this character would become my goal! It might sound crazy, but you have to admit looking at these before and after pictures that it worked! These pictures are proof.

It became clear to me that if I wanted to be something different then what I was, I had to change my thoughts.

37

An important note to keep in mind as you are reading this is that when I developed my character, I did not hold back and limit myself. I didn't consider anything beyond my reach simply because I had no experience or hadn't done it before. My new goal was to overhaul my appearance and get into such great shape that I could appear on the cover of a magazine with my shirt off. I didn't consider that to be far-fetched, unreachable or foolish, even though I was terribly out of shape and about 60 pounds overweight at the time. What I'm saying here is just because you never have doesn't mean you never will.

> I wanted to be a super in shape, handsome, fit, successful guy, but when I looked in the mirror, a 250 pound, overweight, out-of-shape, washed-up jock stared back at me. "How can I get that guy out of here?" I wondered.

When you were reading this, didn't an "ultimate you" character start to appear in your mind (after you got over thinking, "Boy, this guy is a nut case")? Can't you picture this person in your mind's eye? See, it's not so crazy. It's not so hard to do. Getting an image into your mind is a simple first step.

This shouldn't seem so far-fetched—every day business' are built on a vision. Waitresses become star actresses with a vision. So why would it not work to become healthy and fit with a vision?

Get the vision

On that life-changing day as I sat in my kitchen and committed to overhauling my appearance, I thought about the person I wanted to become. I began to construct the character I wanted to be. I created a picture of this person, a sort of visual touchstone. Using a photo from a magazine for guidance, I drew a picture of what I wanted to look like. He was in fantastic shape. He had a sculpted body—a washboard stomach, a defined chest, strong arms. From his bearing it was easy to see that this person was confident. He held his head high. He was strong, healthy, successful and handsome. He was in such peak physical condition that he could have easily been a model for television or magazine advertisements. This was the person I wanted to be.

At the time I felt a little nuts doing this. I kept it well-hidden and probably would have exploded with embarrassment if anyone had seen it. I was a fat college dropout, barely making ends meet. But that didn't matter. This drawing was the person I was to become, and now I had a visual point to focus on. I didn't realize it at the time, but the psychology and peak performance experts have a fancy term for this: "constructive visualization." Looking back, it's a little spooky just how much that drawing resembles the way I look today.

When you make your own visual character image, make it as real as possible. If you can draw, go for it. If not, trace a magazine photo or use software to impose your head on a different body. If you use a magazine

> You can never find what you're not looking for.

photo, however, use a touch of common sense; some professional photos are airbrushed or altered. The image should depict not only the physical traits but also other character traits of your ultimate you.

I not only used this technique on myself, but I use it on my clients, too. When I began training John Mellencamp, he had just experienced a heart attack. The last image the public had of him was as a sickly heart patient. He was preparing to make a comeback, go out on tour again, and I wanted to wipe that hospital-gown image out of everyone's minds. To me this was a rocker who should be leather tough. I wanted him to hit the stage again as the chiseled, hard-hitting, aggressive rock legend he had been before the heart attack. And my training methods supported that tough image of him. My training was hard and aggressive. I was viscous with consistency. Weekends, holidays, we were in the gym. He caught that image for himself and reclaimed it. When he went back out on tour, he blew audiences away. The media made reference to his physical transformation. They described him as "fit as a boxer" and a "lean, mean rocking machine." Heart attack victim? Forget it! This guy will kick your ass!

The mind is the architect of the body. Your body (and your life) will follow where your thoughts lead.

That image, however, wouldn't work for billionaire businessman Bill Cook. The character I used for his overhaul was a commander-in-chief image. His character was energetic, charismatic and full of respect-commanding presence. I pictured him as an admiral at the helm, totally in charge, briskly walking through the halls of the companies he owns, greeting his employees, motivating, inspiring, staying on top of business. Today he is the character I saw him as back when he was in such poor health that doctors didn't expect him to live. I have to admit it feels damn good to have had the privilege to help him make a comeback that shocked everyone, including the medical community.

Burn the New "Ultimate You" Image into your Mind

I had spent years imagining myself as the person I was then—that's how I ended up that way. Think about it. You are who you are because you've spent years thinking of yourself as that person. It was time for me to overwrite that old image with a new one. I had to forget the old image of myself that I had come to accept and burn a new image into my mind. I had to take it from a conscious idea on paper and make it my new subconscious view of myself.

Things quickly began to change for me when I stopped trying to justify my inadequacies.

I took this new image of myself—my ultimate me—and made it my visual mantra. I looked at the picture several times a day. I called up the image in my mind morning, noon and night. Whatever I was doing, I pictured my ultimate me doing it. I had a vision of the ultimate me on the outside, but now I had to internalize it. I had to believe I had the power to change and believe I was the new image that I wanted to be. In other words, I had to believe it to be it.

Bring the Ultimate You to Life

I had created the new image of the person I wanted to become. I had made it my visual mantra. I had internalized the image by burning it into my mind. Then I began to let those internal changes flow out of me by bringing the ultimate me to life.

I'm not talking about being fake or pretending to be someone you're not. On the contrary, by acting like your new image you will be more true to yourself than ever before. James Allen said, "People do not

41

attract that which they want, but that which they are." So now that I had created the identity of who and what I wanted to become, I began mirroring this image. I called this the attitude of become.

Let me explain this attitude of become a little more in depth. Once in an interview, the interviewer asked me why I had been able to succeed at changing my body so drastically when most people who attempt to change their bodies fail. I told the interviewer, "Success in training is dependent upon having the right attitude, the attitude of become. When I decided to get my 250-pound, overweight and out-of-shape body in shape, fit and healthy, the first thing I did was develop this attitude. By definition, 'attitude' means a way of thinking and 'become' means to develop into, assume the form of. It boils down to this: You have to mirror what you want to attract before you can gain it."

I began to think of my character image not as a picture on a paper, but as a person looking in the mirror—my reflection. The ultimate me was attractive, fit and healthy. And I would ask myself, how does an attractive, fit, healthy person act? They eat properly and exercise. So I mirrored that action. The ultimate me was confident. What do confident people do? They speak their minds clearly and know that others will value what they say. I mirrored that action. All the traits I imbued into my ultimate me, I mirrored the actions that would accompany them.

It wasn't a particular exercise or workout routine or miracle supplement or the latest in-vogue diet. My success was the direct result of learning how to get my mind and body to unite and work together.

Most people treat success as something you work to achieve. The attitude of become exposes that fallacy. Success isn't something you pursue, it's something you become. If you see yourself as successful, no matter where you are in life, you will be successful.

Continually Reinforce the Ultimate Me Image

The final step in my transformation from who I was to who I wanted to be was to daily reinforce that I was the ultimate me. I constantly worked to reinforced the idea that I was the attractive, fit, successful person I wanted to be. Continually reinforcing this image made this transformation permanent as opposed to just another broken New Year's resolution.

Purely by accident I came up with this formula: see it, say it, feel it, become it! I used this formula throughout my transformation to daily reinforce the image of my ultimate me. Years later I learned that those smart guys with all the degrees and certificates hanging on the walls in their offices call this visual, auditory and kinesthetic sensory reinforcement.

It's critical that you avoid getting comfortable in a life you don't want.

Continue to visualize yourself as the character image. See yourself as a winner. When you look in the mirror, train yourself to see a positive image. When successful people look in the mirror, they see a success—regardless of what the rest of the world may see on that particular day. Too many people only see a miserable failure staring back at them in the mirror. It's important to know that both images are always there, but you can train yourself to focus on the positive. I have had the honor of training many successful people in many different fields. They all had something in common. They all saw themselves as winners. They knew they were worth something. At one time the world saw them as a pizza delivery boy, a ditch digger and a college dropout. They saw themselves as a rock star and a Fortune 500 CEO and a billionaire, and today the rest of the world shares their view.

Most people are under the illusion that a healthy self-image and a sense of self-worth come after they change their appearance. The big secret is this: It's the other way around.

Auditory reinforcement requires you to take control of your inner dialogue, your thoughts. Practice positive self-talk and eliminate negative thoughts. Chances are if you had a printout of your inner conversation at the end of the day, you would be astounded by the negativity. You would easily see what is holding you back. Each negative statement is a brick in a self-created prison. Don't allow it anymore. When you catch yourself verbally internalizing the thought "I'll always be fat, I'll never lose this weight," stop yourself and replace it with a positive statement about yourself— "I am attractive, healthy and fit."

Kinesthetic reinforcement means to focus on how it feels to be your character image. This includes both physical touch and internal emotions. Begin to feel your character, walk a mile in his shoes. Concentrate on connecting your mind to your body and on feeling attractive, fit, confident. Feel the strength as you build muscles. Enjoy the energy that comes from good nutrition. Bask in the satisfaction of working toward your goals. Relish the freedom you feel from shaking off your negative self-conceptions and inactivity.

A simple explanation of why this all works is that when these seeds are planted firmly in your mind, you will be able to make the right decisions that will guide you along as you pursue your goals. Improving your appearance is directly related to making many decisions on a daily basis. Having a visual goal is like having the blueprints for building a house. The sketch of the completed house is first because it gives everyone the big picture; all the raw materials are then put together to resemble the picture in the sketch.

Conclusion

Many people "diet, workout and exercise," but they don't really make any significant progress or positive change. I didn't want to be one of those people. I always felt that if you were going to do something you might as well do it right. It's easy to go through the motions and just be there, but isn't it smarter to get something back for your effort?

Vigorous exercise is the fountain of youth!

As crazy as all this might sound, what you have read in this chapter is the reason I was so successful. It wasn't a particular exercise or workout routine or miracle supplement or the latest in-vogue diet. My success was the direct result of learning how to get my mind and body to unite and work together.

I'm not a physiologist, but I understand that these steps program your subconscious mind and your subconscious mind is your operating system. Your operating system makes you function. In simple language: you become what you think about. Damn, that sounds easy!

Improving your appearance is directly related to making many decisions on a daily basis.

Most people are under the illusion that a healthy self-image and a sense of self-worth come after they change their appearance. The big secret is this: It's the other way around. The mind is the architect of the body. Your body (and your life) will follow where your thoughts lead. Maybe you don't want to be as into fitness as I am, and maybe being a millionaire isn't what you have in mind, but you do know that where you are now isn't where you want to be. That still small voice is telling you that you can do better. There is a better way to travel than the path you're on. Developing the proper mindset is the first and most important step in lasting change.

46

chapter
it's all about change
3

You have your character image planted firmly in your mind. You are taking steps to make that image grow and flourish. Now let me give you some keys to help with your dramatic change.

Stick with the Ultimate You

Your self-image is the first thing that must change. All other changes spring from this step. Keep doing the things discussed in chapter two. Make that image of the ultimate you second nature. My own amazing transformation was a direct result of changing my self-image.

When people fail in their New Year's resolution to get in shape or lose weight they mistakenly believe they failed because they didn't have enough willpower. They beat themselves up for not trying hard enough, and tell themselves they just don't have what it takes. That is a lie.

In your mind your self-image is in control. It governs all your actions. The truth is that the self-image that you have created with your thoughts has created the person you presently are. Your current self-image is not able to create the new person you wish to become. Your present self-image protects itself and maintains the status quo. No amount of willpower can overcome this self-image, and trying to do so with resolutions and good intentions only produces conflict. (In fact, I've often thought that this is why people consider losing weight a battle.) Resolutions and intentions only allow you to temporarily skip over your present self-image, but pretending that there isn't an elephant in the room doesn't change the fact that it's there. Before long your original thoughts return and the old self-image squashes your good intentions. At the first setback, the old self-image regains control.

To actually succeed at changing yourself, you must first reinvent your self-image so that it is congruent with the new person you wish to become. In other words, you must override the self-image you presently have with the new self-image you wish to change into. It's sort of like upgrading your computer software with a newer version—without the new software the computer cannot perform the new tasks. It can only perform what the old version is programmed to do.

> The truth is that the self-image that you have created with your thoughts has created the person you presently are.

Maybe this sounds like a load of crap to you, but it is your self-image that is the most important tool of change that you have. If you skipped chapter two, either go back and read it or throw this book away. The goal of this book is to help you reinvent yourself and bring this new character image to life. It's hard work. It will take time. But changing your self-image will bring lasting change.

Establish value for yourself

Have you seen the television show where people bring in old stuff that they have sitting around the house to be appraised? Some little old lady brings in a chair that has just been sitting in her spare bedroom for the past 40 years and the appraiser tells her it's actually worth $50,000. She never dreamed it was worth anything, let alone tens of thousands of dollars.

Most people see themselves the same way, and they treat themselves accordingly. They have no idea of their actual worth. When a person says, "I don't have time to exercise," what they are saying is, "I'm not worth the time it takes to exercise." We spend our time and money on what is important to us. The person who won't spend money on their appearance or time on their health is telling the world, "I don't really matter."

This frustrates me. So many amazing people completely undervalue themselves. They treat their pets better than they treat themselves. A race horse receives excellent nutrition and proper exercise. Aren't you every bit as important as a horse? People spend money maintaining their automobiles. They'll wax and buff for hours and only put premium gas in the tank. But many of those same people will fuel themselves with a steady diet of junk food—they eat at the same place their car does! You are a unique, inspiring human being; shouldn't you be treated as well as an inanimate car?

To actually succeed at changing yourself, you must first reinvent your self-image so that it is congruent with the new person you wish to become.

Once I was in Chicago promoting one of my books when Angela and I needed a cab at our hotel. Several cabs were lined up, and the doorman directed us to the first cab in line. I opened the door and saw the dirtiest car I'd ever seen. There was trash everywhere, it smelled, misplaced odds and ends filled the back window. I told the cabby we weren't riding in a dirty cab and asked the doorman for another cab. The cabby was furious and the doorman wanted us to get in just to get the cab driver out of his hair. I wasn't trying to be difficult, but I believe my wife and I are valuable.

I told the doorman and the cab driver, "If we were famous actors or rich business people, you wouldn't dream of asking us to get in a cab that filthy. I am important and so is my wife. We deserve a decent cab."

When I explained it that way, the doorman saw my point. Even the cabby couldn't argue, and he stomped back to his car. The doorman waved up a new cab—this time a clean one—and we were on our way. How about you? Do you see yourself as important as a movie star? Do you think that you have the same worth as a billionaire? You are every bit as valuable as these people—now start acting like it! Your life is priceless! You are worth all the riches in the world, and yet you behave as though you aren't even worth the half an hour it takes to work out or plan a week's worth of nutritious meals.

Sit down and think about your worth. Establish a value for your life. If you had to buy your life, what would you pay for it? When you realize your value, verify it with your behavior.

Understand that appearance does matter

This is another point I have already touched on, but it warrants repeating. I also want to reemphasize it because the idea that looks matter is controversial. I don't want you to just dismiss this truth because you think it's egotistical. Your appearance speaks volumes about who you are.

Why am I making such a fuss about appearance? It's part of bringing out the best in yourself. Your appearance is like a movie screen. It projects you to the world—it's your own billboard advertising who you are. Your self-image, good or bad, is displayed through your appearance. It tells the world just what you believe your value to be.

> Your appearance is like a movie screen. It projects you to the world—it's your own billboard advertising who you are.

I can hear people saying, "Isn't beauty just skin deep?" Yes and no, but my experience tells me that the world responds to appearance. It might not be fair and it might not be right, but that's the way it is. Deal with it. My experience being out of shape and overweight taught me just how much the world values appearance. Remember, I've been there. I once stood where you may now be. That's why I wrote this book. Not to make you obsess over looks, but to help you understand that you are worth the effort.

> When a person says, "I don't have time to exercise," what they are saying is, "I'm not worth the time it takes to exercise."

Quit justifying self-imposed limits

You don't have to be fat simply because the rest of your family is. Don't use your job as an excuse for not exercising. Stop blaming a lack of education for a job that you hate. NO MORE EXCUSES!

I'm over 40 years old. I have two businesses. I write books. I have four kids. I don't have a college degree. I've had knee and shoulder surgeries. If I wanted them, I could have lots of excuses for not pursuing my dreams or for skipping workouts or just letting myself slide. I'd rather have a satisfying life than excuses, wouldn't you?

So many people try to justify their own mediocrity. If you think it's too hard to be your best, fine, just quit trying to blame every one and everything for a decision that is completely yours. Much of mental exercise is pushing yourself out of your own way. When you catch yourself making excuses, stop. Your character image wouldn't accept excuses, so don't you accept them, either. This leads us to our next point ...

No amount of willpower can overcome this self-image, and trying to do so with resolutions and good intentions only produces conflict. (In fact, I've often thought that this is why people consider losing weight a battle.)

You are responsible for you

It seems that when we are faced with responsibility, it's easier to push it off onto someone or something else. We become sort of like children who blame imaginary friends for their wrongdoings. But when we give our power away, we become victims. Giving power away always leads to blame. When we blame others or circumstances, we give up our own sense of responsibility. Many times blame is an attempt to justify our inability to take action and produce results. We look for things outside ourselves to blame for our lack of ability to make things happen. Blame is particularly crippling because it directs control away from the self. It puts someone else in the driver's seat of our lives. Giving your power away is a very dangerous trap.

In all honesty, no circumstance, no person, nothing can really force us to do something without our consent and involvement. But we all seem to fall into this trap from time to time. Success requires that you claim responsibility, stand up and say, "I am in charge here. I am in control. I am responsible for who and what I am. I control my destiny."

The time for an overhaul is now

Have you ever told yourself, "I'll do X when Y happens"? You know what I mean: "I'll start a business when the kids go to school," "I'll exercise every day when I make enough money to afford a gym membership," or "I'll start looking for a better job after I've had time to take some classes." Let me fill you in on a secret: the best time is now. You will never have more time than you have right now. It's true. There will always be something to compete for your time, money and attention.

You are never too old, young, busy, poor, fat, skinny, etc. to start striving for your dreams. Being healthy isn't a privilege set aside for a select few. Stop looking to a time in the future when you think you will be ready and take action now. It is easy to dream about a better you, but not so easy to take the risk and start working toward that goal. Start now. Not tomorrow, not next week, right now.

Don't live your life to please others

When I first met John Mellencamp, I thought, "Boy, is this guy rude." He has no problem speaking his mind. But the more I got to know him, the more I respected that quality in him. No one can say he is a fake. He doesn't have a shred of resentment in his body, and he also accepts the consequences of his outspokenness. He doesn't try to fit in, and he doesn't try to make everyone else happy. He knows that John is responsible for John.

It is easy to dream about a better you, but not so easy to take the risk and start working toward that goal.

If you try to be the person everyone else thinks you should be, you're giving away your self-responsibility. Listen to yourself. Trust yourself. You are unique and created for a purpose—why would you give that up just to please somebody else? Your friends and family might not support your dreams; you need to realize that. But their lack of support doesn't mean your dreams aren't important. It just means it will take them a while to see what you see—and some will see it, some won't.

You see, my definition of success might not be your definition of success. To some, being a millionaire is success. To others Mother Theresa was a success, even though she lived in poverty. You see, success isn't about a dollar amount or a body fat percentage unless that is what matters to you. Success is a relative term, as individual as you are.

To make decisions that are right for you and not just to please others, you have to look inward. Do what you have the desire to do, not what everyone else thinks you should do. If you spend your energies trying to fit other peoples' image of who you should be, you'll never be happy. When other people think you've lost your mind, then you are probably on the right track.

Your friends and family might not support your dreams; you need to realize that.

People thought I was crazy when I walked away from my secure future at Domino's Pizza. People thought I was nuts when I left a six-figure sales job to pursue a full-time writing and consulting career. I can remember my mom asking me when I was going to quit all this crazy weightlifting. They didn't see my version of success. When I was pulling down big paychecks, they thought I was successful, even though I knew it wasn't my dream. All they saw was the risk of leaving those jobs. But now I have achieved my own definition of success, and the same people who thought I was crazy now understand and support my dream.

54

I saw a future where fitness would be a big commodity. I knew I could take fitness from the locker room to the boardroom, and I was right. I help people use fitness in the corporate, entertainment and fashion worlds. When I listened to myself and trusted my dreams, I found I could have both fulfillment and financial security. If I had made my choices trying to please those around me, I would have missed so much. I would have missed achieving my dreams!

> The most strenuous exercise is pushing yourself out of your own way.

Understand the ultimate goal

The ultimate goal of your overhaul is peace of mind. I want to be firm when I point out that being cover-model-beautiful or wearing size-2 jeans or being the best dressed is not the purpose of overhauling your life. I often refer to material examples of success simply because many people can relate to them, but these things in and of themselves are not the ultimate goal.

What you are striving for is peace of mind— being at peace with who you are and knowing you are valuable and full of promise. Pursue fitness and success at the level that brings you happiness. You don't have to have a Ph.D. to take care of your body, look good and be your best. Everything you need is within your grasp. Angela and I are offering a little help and guidance, but ultimately, you are the real expert. You are your best coach, nutritionist, motivator and fashion advisor.

I went on a lot of
diets, ran a bunch
of miles, lifted tons
of weight before I
realized being "fit"
isn't something you pursue;
it's something you become!

2 Rebuild

PART 2

My motivation to get into the gym every day isn't about weight control, six-pack abs or big biceps. My drive comes from the pursuit of personal excellence, a burning desire to avoid complacency.

Chapter 4

Beginner Program

Phase 1—Beginner Level

As I discussed earlier, my objective in writing this book is to share how I overhauled my life. If you can understand the successes and failures I experienced, then you will be able to apply those lessons to your own overhaul. My goal isn't to give you a cookie-cutter workout that would work in theory but be impossible to fit into your lifestyle. I don't know your lifestyle—you do. These are the steps I took.

Twenty years ago, after I had developed the image of the ultimate me and had begun to take the necessary steps to become the successful person I had envisioned, I realized that there were three basic levels of physical fitness: The beginner, intermediate and advanced levels. No matter what your current level of fitness, I recommend starting at the beginner level that I will describe in this chapter—I do. Every year I taper my program back to these beginning exercises. They give me a solid foundation and coming back to them helps me prevent injuries.

As you enter the beginner level of fitness training, always keep your eyes and thoughts on your goal—your ultimate you. You've focused your thoughts and developed the idea of who you were created to be, who you are becoming. So now what do you do with that image? Well, let me tell you what I did . . .

It's ridiculous to think one has to have a
Ph.D. to take care of their body.

So there I was. I was overweight. I was a college dropout. I had a new baby and a wife, and we were struggling from paycheck to paycheck. I had no confidence in myself. Most people would have looked at my situation and written me off, but I had one thing in my favor. I had a vision of the life I wanted to live. I had a new self-image firmly implanted in my mind, and I was changing to become that character. I had already changed my thoughts, and my actions were beginning to change, too.

Millions of people are currently in the same spot I was in then. I had work and family obligations. I didn't have the time to work out. I didn't have the resources to invest in equipment or a gym membership. And I certainly couldn't afford the guidance of a personal trainer—in fact, they didn't even exist then! But I had to do something. My health and my life were worth the price I would need to pay.

Even though I was an ex-athlete, I knew I would have to start from scratch and reinvent my approach to fitness. I couldn't follow my old college football training regimen anymore. I wasn't a college football player. That regimen wouldn't fit my lifestyle or my budget.

> **Even though I was an ex-athlete, I knew I would have to start from scratch and reinvent my approach to fitness.**

To do so would have been doomed from the start. I began investigating body building. I read everything I could get my hands on and evaluated the information. There was so much junk information out there to sift through. Finally, I discovered the key foundation strengthening exercises that I will cover in this chapter. Even now they are the core of my program.

When I knew what exercises were important, I went out and bought an adjustable weight bench and a set of adjustable dumbbells. The equipment cost less than $200, but I had to scrape to pay for it. While relatively inexpensive, the bench and dumbbells were the best choice for me. With them I could work all the basic muscle groups. Having my own equipment also allowed me the flexibility I needed. I could train whenever I had the time, not when the gym was open. That flexibility was a necessity for my busy schedule. I was also somewhat embarrassed to work out in front of others in a gym. I was painfully aware of how out-of-shape I was. The thought of playing the out-of-shape ex-athlete in a gym wore on me. I wanted to build my confidence, not bash it some more. And besides the convenience and the privacy, the

$200 up front was cheaper than a long-term membership contract with monthly payments. Yes, I had to invest something, but it wasn't thousands of dollars. Looking back from where I am now, that hard-scrabble $200 was the best money I ever spent. Those weights have paid for themselves hundreds of times over.

As I began to exercise, though, I made a common mistake. I weighed 250 pounds, and I feared that lifting weights would add to my size, so I concentrated on aerobic exercise to burn fat. I lifted less and less and built up a routine of running six miles a day. I was focused on burning fat, but ignoring the importance of weight training in losing weight and shaping the body. I clung to this routine for several months, but I only lost about 15 pounds, and I was still very flabby. I wasn't shaping my body, I was only a smaller version of what I had been. I didn't feel solid and strong. After my wife had delivered our child, she said she still felt pregnant. That's how I felt. My energy level wasn't good, either. I was tired all the time, my joints were achy, my knees hurt, I felt weak. My exercise program needed adjusting.

Weight lifting allowed me to spend less time training, but was yielding better results.

Even though it was the '80s and running was the exercise all the fitness gurus were pushing, I went my own way. I decided to cut back the mileage and put the weights back in. I lifted weights two to three times a week, working the entire body, and I ran only two to three miles three times a week. I rested for a day or two between each workout. Almost immediately I started to physically change. It just clicked. I began to notice in my own body some of the characteristics from the ultimate me I had drawn.

I realized how important weight lifting really was. It dawned on me that in training, less can be more. Weight lifting allowed me to spend less time training, but was yielding better results.

In the beginning, I knew my past eating habits weren't good, but I didn't obsess about nutrition. My goal was simply to eat better. I didn't follow any crazy diets or bury myself in books on nutrition. I just tried to apply some common sense to what I was eating. I cut back slowly. It sounds funny now, but instead of eating a whole pizza, I just ate a couple pieces. I tried to get plenty of lean meats and vegetables. I cut back on the alcohol and the fast food. I always ate breakfast. My old habits were pretty bad, so the simple steps I took were a big improvement.

Most people who embark upon a fitness program make the mistake of trying to adapt themselves to the fitness lifestyle. What made me successful was that I adapted fitness to fit my lifestyle, even in my eating habits. When you try to change to a drastically different lifestyle, it causes conflict. That's why so many people drop out of a program. As I moved into the intermediate and advanced stages of fitness, I learned much more about nutrition, but early on I tried to eat in moderation. And as I noticed the way eating better improved my concentration and energy, I was encouraged to continue eating better.

For those of you who really struggle with food issues, I don't mean to gloss over nutrition in the beginning phase. Believe me, having grown up in an Italian home where everything revolves around food and lots of it, I understand your fight. But you have to hang on to your ultimate you image. The person in that picture wouldn't drown their problems in a bag of Oreos—and that is the person you are becoming. You are mirroring the actions of that character, that person who represents the best that is in you. The old you may have eaten to the point of self-loathing, but you have already decided you are now a fit, successful person—so act like it! Remember, the majority of my transformation didn't take place in the gym, but in my mind.

As I continued to focus on my visual mantra of my ultimate me and as my body firmed up, my long-missing confidence was resurfacing. I believed I could change my life, and as I did, my confidence rose. At the beginner level I kept the mental aspect simple. I continued to reinforce my image of the ultimate me, and every day I was becoming that image. I continued to see myself as successful, I eliminated negative thoughts and replaced them with positive self-talk, and I enjoyed feeling my body grow stronger and the growing self-confidence I had found.

People who see my before and after photos are often shocked to realize that the program I began with is so simple. Actually, pleasantly surprised is a better way to describe their reaction. It didn't take lots of money. It only took about eight hours a week. I didn't need tons of special equipment or a degree in nutrition or therapy to dissect my childhood. The fitness industry has overcomplicated the simple concept of living a healthy life. As long as you are confused about

The fitness industry has overcomplicated the simple concept of living a healthy life.

fitness, you'll continue to pay fitness gurus money! They don't want you to understand. But my common sense approach is very doable for anyone. I focused the majority of my efforts on the mental aspect of transformation, then I lifted weights, did some aerobic work, and tried to eat better. I did what fit into my quickly-improving lifestyle, and the results were even better than I imagined.

The Phase 1 Beginner Level Program

Beginning my new training program was exciting, but also a little confusing. It was also uncomfortable and challenging at times, so I devoted my first few training sessions to starting simple and familiarizing myself with the exercises, routine and techniques that I had decided to use. I was very careful to keep in mind that I was just starting out and not judge my exercising ability by these initial workouts. I was also careful to remember that I would be using muscles that I hadn't used in a long time. I didn't expect myself to perform all of the exercises perfectly, lift the heaviest weights, or run the full distance in the beginning.

I was very careful to keep in mind that I was just starting out and not judge my exercising ability by these initial workouts.

As I mentioned, I bought a set of adjustable dumbbells, an adjustable weight bench, an inexpensive stationary exercise bike, and I set those up in the corner of my apartment. Not expensive or fancy, but, boy, did it work!

I decided that working out three times a week would work best for me. This fit best with my work and family obligations. My training schedule was Monday-Wednesday-Friday. Each workout session included cardiovascular exercise mixed with weight training. I worked my whole body during each session. Each session lasted 60 to 90 minutes. Though some people choose to do one type of training per workout, combining cardiovascular training with weight training saved me time. I also discovered it promoted faster weight loss and prevented over training and burnout.

The basic structure of my program was an aerobic warm-up, weight training, then an aerobic cool-down. For the aerobic warm-up I rode a stationary bike at a fairly easy pace for 10 minutes. Once I warmed up, I moved to the weight training part of the workout which is explained in the next few pages. After weight training I rode the bike again.

Weight Training Exercises

For weight training to be effective, you must perform it properly. An important rule to remember is that more is not always better. The goal in weight training should not be to build huge muscles so that you can kick sand in somebody's face. The goal should be to develop your muscles in a well-balanced, symmetrical manner. This is why I focused on developing a balance of strength, muscle mass, muscle tone, shape, definition, symmetry and endurance. During this initial phase I found I got the best results by focusing on basic movements using the pyramid technique. Let me explain both of these terms.

There two classifications of weight-training exercises: basic and isolation. Basic exercises stress the largest muscle groups of the body, often in combination with smaller muscles. Typical basic movements include bench presses, shoulder presses, barbell arm curls and leg presses. Isolation exercises stress a single muscle group or part of a single muscle in relative isolation from the rest of the body. Isolation exercises are good for shaping and defining muscle groups. Two examples of isolation exercises that help shape and define the thighs are leg extensions and leg curls.

The goal should be to develop your muscles in a well-balanced, symmetrical manner.

Pyramid sets enable you to train with heavy weights in a progressive or pyramid manner. Muscle fibers grow and get stronger by contracting against resistance. It isn't wise to just jump in and begin lifting heavy weights, but by practicing the pyramid technique you can add weight progressively as you go through the workout. I performed 3 sets, increasing the weight 5-10 lbs each set.

The first set I used a weight that allowed me to perform around 12 repetitions. The second set I used a weight that allowed me to perform 10 reps and the third set I used a weight that allowed me to perform 8 reps.

As I said, during most of this phase I followed basic exercises, but did add in isolation exercises for my neck and lower back: the four-way neck isometrics and the floor hyperextensions. When I first started my program I found that when I did my abdominal work my neck really felt weak and hurt me. A couple of sessions doing the neck isometric exercises, my neck quickly strengthened up and the discomfort and pain disappeared.

65

Specific training techniques require different rest periods between reps. Your current condition will dictate how much rest you need between sets. As you get into better shape, the need for rest will decrease. A good rule to follow is when you just start to recover your breath, begin the next set. It will help you work at your current level of conditioning. As you get into better shape, the rest period adjusts naturally because the better condition you're in, the faster you recover.

And speaking of breathing, when performing a weight lifting movement, I simply recommend that you breath in a way that is natural for you. An easy way to synchronize your breathing pattern is to inhale as you lower the weight and say "ooh" or "ahhh" as you raise the weight. Making that funny little sound will force you to exhale and prevent you from holding your breath.

After an effective training session, your body needs time to recover. For instance, when you lift weights, you actually tear down muscle cells. If you feed those cells the right nutrients and provide a proper recovery period, the muscle cells will rebuild themselves bigger and stronger than they were before. If you do not allow enough time for this rebuilding process, you will not get the full benefits of training. Working out too often, or for too long, actually hinders the body's recuperative abilities.

Terms You Should Know

Cardiovascular or aerobic exercise:

Exercises such as jogging that, although strenuous, are rhythmical and performed at less than all-out intensity allowing you to safely elevate your heart rate to a level that produces cardiovascular benefit. This level is called the aerobic training zone or target zone.

Exercise:

Each individual movement performed in your routine.

Repetition or reps:

One complete lifting movement. You perform one rep of an arm curl, for example, by holding free weights in each hand with your arms down by your sides, contracting your arm muscles and raising the weights forward toward your shoulders, then lowering them back to the starting position at your sides. Reps are the number of completed lifting movements from start to finish.

Set:

A number of reps completed in succession. For example, if you perform 10 complete reps of arms curls, rest for a moment, then perform 10 more reps of arms curls, you will have completed two full sets.

Rest interval:
The recovery time between reps and sets. It can last from 30 seconds to five minutes.

Weight:
The actual pounds lifted or pressed.

Lifting motion:
The plains of travel or arcs of movement. There are two plains of travel: the concentric positive portion of movement and the eccentric negative portion. During the concentric positive part of a lift, the muscle shortens as it develops tension to overcome the resistance. During the eccentric negative portion, the muscle lengthens while developing tension. In the arm curl exercise, the downward part of the lift is the eccentric part. You don't have to remember these terms; just concentrate on the positive and the negative portions of a lift. Make sure that the negative portion is slow. You want to be in control of the weight enough to feel it when it goes up and to control it as it comes down. Many people only get half of the benefit of an exercise because they only concentrate on the positive portion of a lift.

You want to be in control of the weight enough to feel it when it goes up and to control it as it comes down.

Feel:
The sensation you get in your muscles as you perform an exercise. Tightness, firmness, swelling and burning are all good reactions to resistance training. The most important feeling is the pump. That is the swollen feeling you get in your muscle toward the end of a set. Muscle pump is caused by the rapid movement of blood into the muscles to remove fatigue toxins while replacing supplies of fuel and oxygen. When you succeed at creating a good muscle pump, you have worked a muscle or muscle group optimally. Burn is caused by a rapid build up of fatigue toxins in a muscle and is a good indication that you have worked a muscle or muscle group optimally. Extending repetitions past the pump stage will produce a burn.

After the 10 minute warm-up I described earlier, I was ready to go through the weights. I arranged my exercises according to body parts: chest, back, shoulders, biceps, triceps, legs, calves, abdominals, lower back and neck. I began my weight training exercise following this order:

1. Dumbbell Chest Press on a Flat Bench (chest)

The most popular exercise for the chest and upper body for good reason. This exercise primarily stresses the chest muscles but also puts a secondary emphasis on the front of the shoulders and the back of the arms.

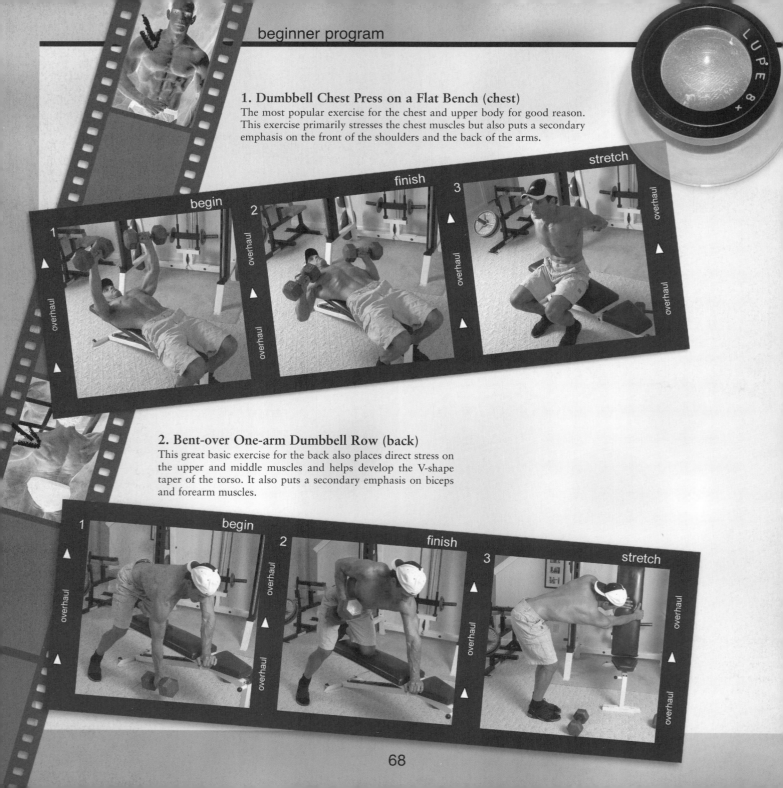

2. Bent-over One-arm Dumbbell Row (back)

This great basic exercise for the back also places direct stress on the upper and middle muscles and helps develop the V-shape taper of the torso. It also puts a secondary emphasis on biceps and forearm muscles.

68

3. Dumbbell Shoulder Press (shoulders)

The best exercise for the shoulders involves pressing a weight overhead, which stresses the entire shoulder girdle and puts a secondary stress on the back of the arms (triceps).

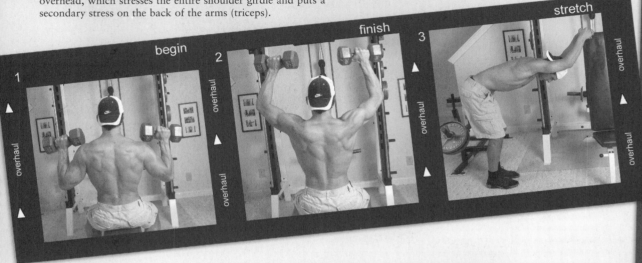

4. Dumbbell Arm Curl (biceps)

This exercise involves curling a dumbbell in a semicircular arc up to a position just beneath the chin then, without pausing, slowly lowering to the front of the hips.

69

5. Bench Dip (triceps)

A great fundamental exercise for the triceps. I performed 3 sets of 12-15 reps using just my body weight.

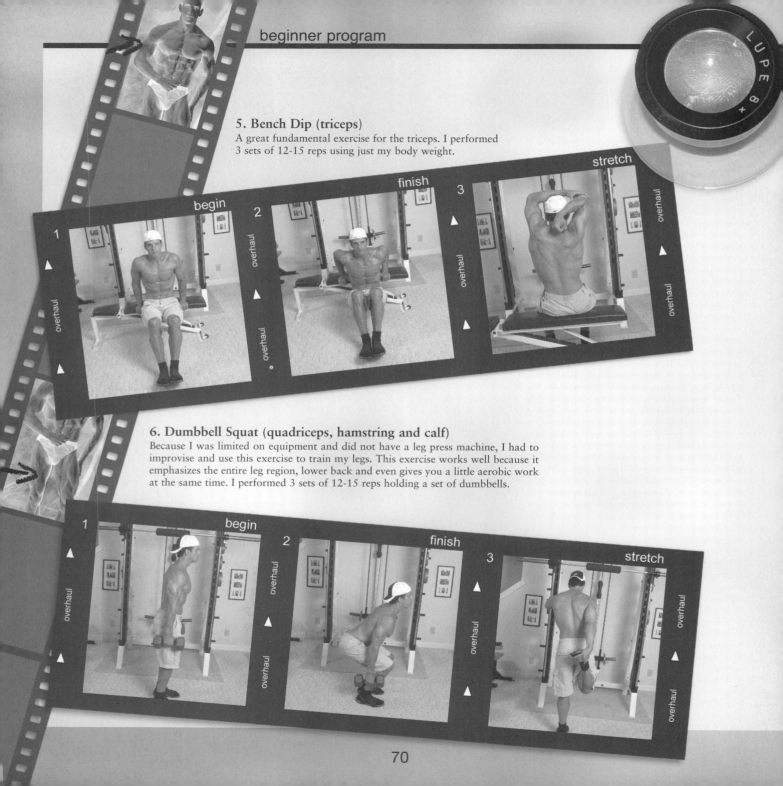

6. Dumbbell Squat (quadriceps, hamstring and calf)

Because I was limited on equipment and did not have a leg press machine, I had to improvise and use this exercise to train my legs. This exercise works well because it emphasizes the entire leg region, lower back and even gives you a little aerobic work at the same time. I performed 3 sets of 12-15 reps holding a set of dumbbells.

7. Dumbbell One-leg Calf Raise (calf)

This exercise required that I use a step. Calf exercises are often left out of beginning weight training programs, but they shouldn't be. The calves are important for performance and body symmetry. The standing calf raise is the most basic exercise for shaping the calves.

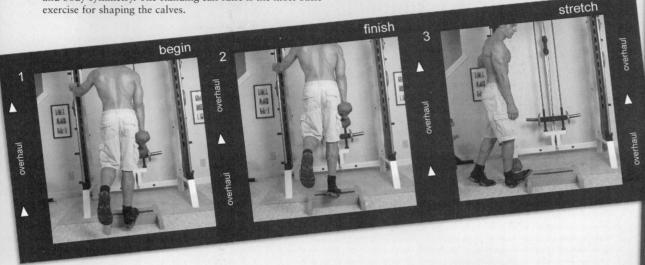

8. Partial Incline Sit-up (abdominals)

The partial incline sit-up is "partial" because you do not go through a full range of motion when performing this exercise. I found it best to use only the upper 65 percent of the movement, which alleviates stress on the lower back. What's great about this exercise is that when performed correctly, it stresses the upper and lower abdominal with no pressure or pain in the lower back. I performed 3 sets of 12-15 reps using just my body weight.

9. Floor Hyperextensions (back)

My lower back had been bothering me for some time before I began my program. I knew that my lower back being weak would eventually become a big problem if I didn't strengthen it proportionally with the rest of my body. The floor hyperextension exercise proved to be excellent for strengthening my lower back, helping to eliminate pain and discomfort. It is easy, safe, requires no equipment and can be performed anywhere. I performed 3 sets of 12-15 reps using just my body weight.

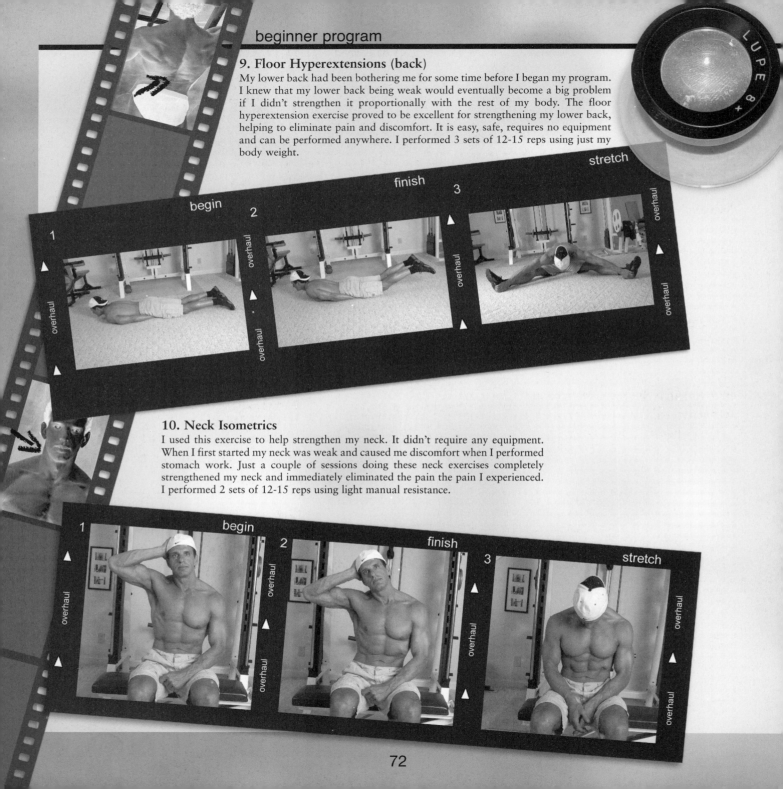

10. Neck Isometrics

I used this exercise to help strengthen my neck. It didn't require any equipment. When I first started my neck was weak and caused me discomfort when I performed stomach work. Just a couple of sessions doing these neck exercises completely strengthened my neck and immediately eliminated the pain the pain I experienced. I performed 2 sets of 12-15 reps using light manual resistance.

After completing all the exercises, I would get back on my stationary bike or go out for a jog for 20 to 30 minutes of moderate pace aerobic exercise. I found this to be beneficial for two reasons—it helped burn body fat and start the recovery process.

My main goal when I began training was to get used to the routine. I needed to start from scratch and familiarize myself with the exercise movements. For me it worked best that I train three times per week with weights with a day or two of rest between each workout. This routine seemed to allow me to slowly break into the new activities without allowing them to get in the way overwhelming my lifestyle at the time. Something else might work better for you. Your lifestyle and your goals will be factors in determining the routine you select. The important thing to remember in establishing your routine is to be comfortable with it and to make sure that it fits your lifestyle. Setting up a routine that is wrong for you can cause conflict and anxiety which, in turn, usually lead to skipping workouts and eventually an end to your training.

"Your lifestyle and your goals will be factors in determining the routine you select."

Time to move on

After progressing through this phase, I started to see signs of success. I began to feel stronger, more energetic and enthusiastic. I was looking more fit and athletic. I felt more in control of my life (and I was), and this control gave me more confidence. I was feeling more alert, ambitious and more eager to face challenges.

I was happy with myself that throughout this phase of training I was patient, eager to learn, open to experiment, persistent, and dedicated to my program, but ...

After about eight weeks I was getting bored with it all. I was starting to see diminished results, develop some miner aches and pains, my motivation was starting to wane, which signaled to me that needed to make a change. I had mastered this phase of training and needed to challenge myself further. My body had changed, my lifestyle had changed, my outlook had changed, and now my program needed to change. The pressures of supporting a family, work, a new baby in the house, trying to fit exercise in and eat right caught up and overwhelmed me. I felt it was time to regroup. Here's what I did.

I decided to give myself a little test and see if this was truly something I wanted to continue. I made a list on a piece of paper with two headings: "If my body stays the same" and "If I rebuild my body." Then I made a list of what was important in my life—career, social life, family and so forth. I asked myself this question, "Will I be happy with my (filled in the blank from my list)?" "If my body stays the same?" Then, I did the same thing but ended with the other question, "If I develop my body?"

My answers on my list provided me with the answer I needed to get me going again. Seeing the results of this test helped me make decisions more easily. This also showed me I needed to make some trade-offs, adjustments and to be open to change. Of course, I couldn't rebuild my body with little effort. Rebuilding it required giving up that which didn't support my goal for that which did. This little test sure made the choices easier for me to make and led me to the next phase of my training which I will cover in chapter 5.

You're probably shocked at the simplicity and humbleness of this program. It was the simplicity that made it the perfect gateway into the next phase you will read about in the next chapter. Change is never easy, but it's too easy with fitness and weight loss to needlessly put a mountain in front of you.

Chapter

5

Intermediate program

Phase 2-Intermediate Level

Some people can maintain a beginner level program for the rest of their lives. They never get bored with it, and they always find challenge in their weekly training sessions. I, however, wasn't one of those people. After several months of training at the beginner level, I began to worry about maintaining my fitness. I was thrilled with my confidence and energy levels, and it was easy to see I looked better, but I was getting bored. Work was the emphasis in working out. I was dreading training, and I was frustrated by my lack of progress. In Phase 1, I had realized that getting in shape wasn't just a one-time event; it was a whole lifestyle overhaul—but how could I stay focused? I didn't want to give up the benefits of training, but I wasn't sure how to stay interested. I struggled for a while before I realized that I needed to make changes.

The answer was to challenge myself again. I had to evolve. Humans are always changing. We're either getting better or getting worse. I couldn't just keep doing the same thing and continue to improve. It is at this same point that many people begin to backslide in a fitness program that has previously afforded them great success. They never reevaluate their programs or challenge themselves, and they quietly begin to slack off and miss workouts or eat worse or return to their old bad habits.

I decided I wanted to keep going, so I asked myself, "What's the next step?" I went back and did some more investigating.

I discovered that the weights were doing more than the running, so I focused on developing the weight training portion of my program. The results of my beginner program were terrific: weight loss, muscle tone, improved circulation, increased strength and energy and more relaxed sleep. But I wanted to fine-tune my physical appearance further and achieve a greater level of fitness. While keeping the key exercises from the beginner level, I began to add more muscle-specific shaping exercises. These exercises added definition to my body. In order to perform some of these exercises, though, I needed more than my trusty old weight bench.

Joining a gym might be the best fit for you. If not, you might want to consider purchasing equipment. As I progressed through the intermediate phase of my training, I found a company that manufactured quality home equipment. I prefer the PTS Home Training System by Pro Industries. In fact, it's the equipment you see in all the exercise photos in this book. Safety was a big issue for me since I worked out by myself, this equipment offers hundreds of exercise options and all the advantages of free weights and machines combined without the need for a spotter.

The Phase 2— Intermediate Level Program

I was ready to add new basic and isolation exercises to better develop each body part. But when I tried to add them to the workout I was following in phase one, the routine became too much to confront in a single session. I was still working my entire body each session as I had done at the beginner level, but as my technique improved, I worked each muscle group more intensely. Working all of my body each session was overtraining me. I needed longer periods of rest between working muscle groups.

I decided to keep my weight training schedule Monday, Wednesday and Friday, but to split up my workouts by muscle groups. On Monday I worked my chest, shoulders, triceps and abdomen; on Wednesday I worked my legs and abdomen; and on Friday I worked by back, biceps,

> **I discovered that the weights were doing more than the running, so I focused on developing the weight training portion of my program.**

forearms and abdomen. I kept the cardio portion of my program about the same, running 2-3 miles three days a week. The new schedule allowed me to increase the number of weight training exercises per body part and allowed me to focus more attention on fine-tuning without overtraining. And the new routine didn't increase the time I spent working out. Each session still lasted 60-90 minutes.

This change in my program produced immediate results and revived my interest. But I still needed to do some fine-tuning. I was still a little achy and not losing the body fat the way I wanted to. That's when I discovered the magic recipe. I had been running first, then lifting weights. I learned that when we exercise, we burn stored energy in the first 30 minutes, then we burn the secondary source of energy—body fat. The way I had been doing it, I might have done 40 minutes of cardio work but only 10 minutes of that was actually burning body fat. So I changed to a 10-minute warm-up, weights, then running. By lifting weights first, I used stored energy for weights, but all of my aerobic work used body fat. The inches started to come off in all the right places and increased definition of my muscles brought me closer and closer to the ultimate me.

Weight Training Exercises

I continued to use the weight training exercises I used at the beginning level, but I added the following exercises to my workout.

This change in my program produced immediate results and revived my interest.

77

LUPE 8

MONDAY'S
ROUTINE

CHEST
1. Smith Machine Chest Press
I performed 3 sets increasing the weight 5-10 lbs each set. The first set I used a weight that allowed me to perform around 12 reps. The second set I performed 10 reps, and the third set I performed 8 reps.

begin
finish
stretch

1 2 3

overhaul

2. Dumbbell Incline Bench Chest Press
I performed 3 sets increasing the weight 5-10 lbs each set. The first set I used a weight that allowed me to perform around 12 reps. The second set I performed 10 reps, and the third set I performed 8 reps.

begin
finish
stretch

1 2 3

overhaul

The Chest
In order to continue to develop my chest, I needed to begin working on my upper chest. That meant adding an additional basic exercise: the incline chest press. To work on my chest definition, I added an isolation exercise: the dumbbell flat bench fly. Dumbbell flys will give muscle detail creating shape and enhancing symmetry and tone.

Chest Anatomy
The chest, or pectoral muscle, is composed of two fan-like muscles that cover the rib cage. Their function is to push the body away from an object or surface and to pull the arms across the front of the body.

3. Dumbbell Flat Bench Fly

I performed 3 sets increasing the weight 5-10 lbs each set. The first set I used a weight that allowed me to perform around 12 reps. The second set I performed 10 reps, and the third set I performed 8 reps.

SHOULDERS
1. Smith Machine Shoulder Press

I performed 3 sets increasing the weight 5-10 lbs each set. The first set I used a weight that allowed me to perform around 12 reps. The second set I performed 10 reps, and the third set I performed 8 reps.

The Shoulders

Pressing a weight overhead remained my primary exercise for the shoulders. However, in order to further develop and define the muscle group, I added the dumbbell lateral raise exercise.

Shoulder Anatomy

The shoulder muscle is composed of three muscles called the deltoids. The deltoids move the arm forward, backward, to the side, up and around. In order to perform these movements, the deltoids have three lobes of muscle called heads (the muscle in front called the anterior head, the muscle on the side called the medial head, and the muscle in the rear called the posterior head).

MONDAY'S
ROUTINE

2. Dumbbell Lateral Raises

I performed 3 sets increasing the weight 5-10 lbs each set. The first set I used a weight that allowed me to perform around 12 reps. The second set I performed 10 reps, and the third set I performed 8 reps.

The Abdomen

The abdominals are a group of muscles that are the visual center of the body. More than any other muscle group, they help define how fit you are. I divide the abdominals into three areas: the upper, lower and sides.

ABDOMEN

1. Crunches (upper abdominal)

I performed 3 sets of 12-15 reps.

MONDAY'S ROUTINE

ABDOMEN
2. Seated Incline Knee-ups (lower abdominal)
I performed 3 sets of 12-15 reps.

begin

2 finish

3 stretch

Abdomen Anatomy
The abdominal muscles pull the upper body (the rib cage) and the lower body (the pelvis) toward each other, and they help to keep the internal organs in place. The rectus abdominis, a long muscle extending along the length of the ventral aspect of the abdomen, is the muscle that flexes and draws the sternum toward the pelvis. The external obliques are muscles at each side of the torso, commonly called the "love handles," that rotate the spinal column. The intercostals, two thin planes of muscular and tendon fibers that occupy the spaces between the ribs, lift the ribs and draw them together.

3. Broom Stick Twist (sides)
I performed 1 set of 50-70 reps.

begin

2

3 finish

WEDNESDAY'S ROUTINE

LEGS

1. Leg Press
I performed 3 sets increasing the weight 5-10 lbs each set. The first set I used a weight that allowed me to perform around 12 reps. The second set I performed 10 reps, and the third set I performed 8 reps.

begin 1

2 finish

3 stretch

2. Leg Extension
I performed 3 sets increasing the weight 5-10 lbs each set. The first set I used a weight that allowed me to perform around 12 reps. The second set I performed 10 reps, and the third set I performed 8 reps.

begin 1

2 finish

3 stretch

The Legs
In the first phase of my program I was somewhat limited by my lack of equipment on what I could do with my legs. Two machines I added to my home gym—the leg press and the combination leg extension/leg curl machine—gave me lots of new exercise options. These machines are also available at most gyms. The most basic exercise for the legs is the leg press. It is great for stressing the muscles from the waist down. The leg press emphasizes the entire lower body with specific emphasis on the quadriceps. Leg extensions are great for defining and shaping the front of the thigh, especially the knee area. This exercise is performed on a leg extension machine. The leg extension emphasizes the front of the thighs/quadricep muscles. Probably the most underdeveloped muscle in the lower body region is the hamstring (back of the thigh). The best way to develop the hamstring muscle is the lying leg curl. This exercise directly emphasizes the back of the leg/hamstring muscles.

WEDNESDAY'S ROUTINE

3. Leg Curls

I performed 3 sets increasing the weight 5-10 lbs each set. The first set I used a weight that allowed me to perform around 12 reps. The second set I performed 10 reps, and the third set I performed 8 reps.

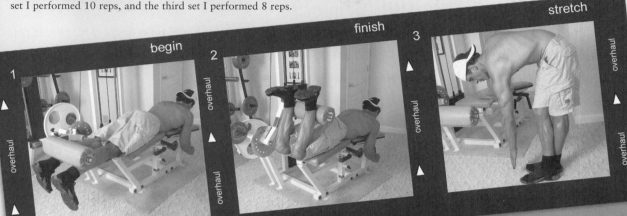

Leg Anatomy

The leg can be divided into two areas, the upper portion and the lower portion. The upper leg, the thigh, is made up of the quadriceps. These muscles are at the front of the thigh and work to extend and straighten the leg. Also located in the upper leg just opposite the quadriceps are the hamstring muscles which help to curl the leg back. The hamstrings are sometimes called the leg biceps. The lower leg, located below the knee, is made up of the calves which flex the foot.

4. Standing Calf Raise

I performed 3 sets increasing the weight 5-10 lbs each set. The first set I used a weight that allowed me to perform around 12 reps. The second set I performed 10 reps, and the third set I performed 8 reps.

BACK
1. Lat Machine Pull-downs
I performed 3 sets increasing the weight 5-10 lbs each set. The first set I used a weight that allowed me to perform around 12 reps. The second set I performed 10 reps, and the third set I performed 8 reps.

FRIDAY'S ROUTINE

begin
finish
stretch

2. Seated Low Pulley Cable Rows
I performed 3 sets increasing the weight 5-10 lbs each set. The first set I used a weight that allowed me to perform around 12 reps. The second set I performed 10 reps, and the third set I performed 8 reps.

begin
finish
stretch

The Back
The back muscles cover a large territory and are the largest muscles in the upper body. These muscles stretch from the base of the neck to the top of the butt and go from shoulder to shoulder. In the beginning, I found my back difficult to train because I was unable to feel the muscles when I performed the repetitions. My arms seemed to be doing all the work. Lightening the weight and focusing on slowing down the reps helped me better isolate my back muscles. With my new equipment I was able to add the pull-down exercise and the seated cable row which are two of the best overall back exercises. For my lower back I stuck with the hyperextension exercise.

3. Lower Back Extension

I performed 3 sets increasing the weight 5-10 lbs each set. The first set I used a weight that allowed me to perform around 12 reps. The second set I performed 10 reps, and the third set I performed 8 reps.

BICEP
1. Barbell Arm Curl

I performed 3 sets increasing the weight 5-10 lbs each set. The first set I used a weight that allowed me to perform around 12 reps. The second set I performed 10 reps, and the third set I performed 8 reps.

Back Anatomy

The back muscles are composed of the trapezius—the flat triangular muscle that extends out and down from the neck and down between the shoulder blades. The trapezius raises the shoulder girdle and the latissimus dorsi or lats—the large triangular muscles that extend from under the shoulders down to the small of the back on both sides. The lats pull the shoulders downward, and the spinal erectors—the muscles in the lower back that guard the nerve channels and help to keep the spine erect—straighten the spine from a position of a flexed torso completely forward and help arch the lower and middle back.

The Biceps

The best and most basic way to train the biceps is using a barbell. I took advantage of my adjustable bench to do incline dumbbell curls. To give my biceps some variety I purchased a barbell with adjustable collars.

85

FRIDAY'S ROUTINE

2. Incline Dumbbell Arm Curl

I performed 3 sets increasing the weight 5-10 lbs each set. The first set I used a weight that allowed me to perform around 12 reps. The second set I performed 10 reps, and the third set I performed 8 reps.

begin — 1
finish — 2
stretch — 3

FOREARM

To give my arms balance and to help strengthen my grip, I added in the barbell wrist curl exercise.

1. Wrist Curl With Barbell

I performed 3 sets of 12-15 reps with the same weight.

Bicep Anatomy
The arm muscles are divided into three areas: biceps, triceps and forearm. The bicep (bicep brachii) is a two-headed muscle that starts under the deltoid with its point of insertion below the elbow. The bicep lifts and curls the arm and twists the arm downward.

Forearm anatomy
The forearm is composed of a variety of muscles on the outside and inside of the lower arm that control the actions of the hand and wrist. The forearm flexor muscles curl the palm down and forward. The forearm extensor muscles curl the knuckles back and up.

begin — 1
finish — 2
stretch — 3

The Abdomen
Repeat Monday's workout.
For variety I mixed up the order, starting with the last exercise in the sequence first.

Getting serious about stretching

In beginner phase of my program I dabbled a little with stretching—once in while after my workout I would sit on the ground and do a few of the leg stretches that I remembered from my football days. But as I was getting into better shape, it became evident that I had lost a fair amount of the flexibility that I once had as an athlete. The poor condition I had gotten into coupled with the aging process left me stiff and inflexible.

Wanting to get more flexible I studied the benefits of stretching a little more deeply. Most injuries are caused by the overextension of a joint, muscle, or connective tissue creating pulled muscles, sprains and strains. I understood stretching improved athletic ability, balance, agility and speed, and I had always realized that stretching was good for preventing injuries. But something that I did not know was how stretching can help add definition, shape and contour to the body. Stretching can be used to enhance the appearance of the body. In the next phase I will show you how I implemented stretching into my program that helped not only prevent injuries but really helped me fine-tune my body while at the same time helping me to pace my workouts, speed recovery and give me amazing flexibility.

But something that I did not know was how stretching can help add definition, shape and contour to the body.

Nutrition

It was during Phase 2 that I stopped eating whatever sounded good and started eating for performance. It was still the '80s and people were counting calories like crazy. While eating a certain number of calories would probably help me lose weight, I felt that wasn't the solution. Common sense told me that 2500 calories from candy wouldn't give me the same effect as 2500 calories from meat or 2500 calories from vegetables, so again I began to investigate food and what different foods provided my body.

I started to break nutrition down. I realized that all foods fall into three basic categories: carbohydrates, proteins and fats. I asked, "What are carbohydrates? What do they do? What are proteins? What are fats? What do they give my body?" I wanted to learn what each group did for my body and learn to eat around that. So what does each type of food do? Well, let me give you the quickie overview.

Carbohydrates give us energy. That doesn't mean, however, that the more carbs you eat, the more energetic you are. Carbs are broken down into two groups, complex carbohydrates—oatmeal, grains, breads, rice, pasta and potatoes—and simple carbohydrates—fruits, sugars and honey. I eat mainly complex carbohydrates. I take it easy on the simple carbs, and I try to avoid simple carbohydrates with processed sugar, such as cookies and other sweets.

The body uses protein to build, repair and maintain muscle tissue. To me, it seemed that proteins were very important to what I was trying to do with my body, even though the diets of the day discouraged eating meat. Protein is made up of amino acids. The body can't use the protein unless all of the necessary amino acids are present. Some protein foods contain all the essential amino acids, some don't. Milk, eggs, meat, fish and soybeans are examples of complete protein foods. Vegetables are an example of incomplete protein foods. I strive for a mixture of the two types.

Fats get a lot of bad press, but our body needs them. Fat provides the body with stored energy, cushions vital organs, carries the fat-soluble vitamins A, D, E and K and insulates the body from excessive cold by preserving body heat. Fats are broken down into saturated and unsaturated. Saturated fats such as butter and lard are derived mainly from animal sources and they can contribute to clogged arteries. I consume mainly unsaturated fats from nuts and seeds and vegetable oils. Unsaturated fats break down into polyunsaturated and monounsaturated, but I don't worry too much about that. If it's a fat that hardens at room temperature, I avoid it.

Keeping track of how what I ate made me feel really helped me listen to my body and identify the ratio of food from each group that I needed to be my best.

Obviously, there is more to nutrition than what I gave you in those three paragraphs, but you don't need a Ph.D. to figure out what to eat for breakfast. My book **Body Mastery** goes into greater detail about nutrition if you are interested in learning more. Once I learned what those basic types of food did for my body, I began to experiment. I started a journal. I began to write down everything I ate and the effect of that food on my body. I kept track of what I ate, when I ate it, where I ate it, and how it made me feel. By keeping track of when and where I ate, I was able to identify unhealthy habits such as eating a fatty drive-through meal in the car or a sugary vending machine snack. Better planning helped me rectify those situations. Keeping track of how what I ate made me feel really helped me listen to my body and identify the ratio of food from each group that I needed to be my best.

Back then nutritionists touted a low-fat "runner's diet" loaded with complex carbohydrates. I didn't feel so good on that diet. I felt groggy and grumpy. I thought, "Fats can't be all bad. I need fat for good hair, nails and skin. And I need protein to build muscles." I knew I needed carbs for energy, but with the high carbs, I wasn't feeling so energetic. I needed balance. So I began to cut back on the pastas and add lean meats, which also added fat. I began to perk up. In the morning my meal included both carbs and proteins, with an emphasis on carbs to provide energy for the day. At lunch I ate a balance of carbs and proteins. If I needed energy, I often had a light afternoon snack. For supper I again had carbs and protein, but with the emphasis now on protein. I needed the protein then because the body rebuilds itself during sleep. At night I cut back on the carbs, even so-called good carbs, because I didn't need energy while I slept and that unused energy would only be converted to fat. Basically my intake of carbohydrates and protein flip-flopped from morning to evening, and since I was eating lean meats, I was still getting the fats I needed without overdoing it.

> At night I cut back on the carbs, even so-called good carbs, because I didn't need energy while I slept and that unused energy would only be converted to fat.

I didn't have nutrition mastered, but I was getting better—and looking and feeling better. I was discovering that there was a formula to eating for performance. I was taking control of my diet in a way that I had never done before. Instead of just showing up and eating whatever was served to me, I began to think ahead: "If the cafeteria is serving a fatty lunch, I need to bring something from home. If I have to be at the office early, what do I need to do to get breakfast in?" Some people consider this too much effort, or that they would be slaves to nutrition. To the contrary, eating this way was very freeing. I was no longer controlled by the latest diet, now I ate what made my body and mind perform at their best.

Staying motivated

In Phase 2 I began to set goals for my body. I set goals for myself in my career and in my finances, but never for my body. I completely abandoned the most common goal-setting device—the scales. I didn't care so much about how much I weighed as long as I looked and felt good. The scale didn't distinguish between losing body fat and gaining muscle mass. Instead, I set long-term goals. I had a picture in my mind of how I wanted to look when I was 30, 40, 50 and beyond. I backed that goal up with mid-range and short-term goals such as a goal for the year and a goal for each season. By using long-, mid-, and short-range goals I could easily see where I was going and what I needed to do to get there.

For some time I cruised along in the intermediate phase. I was looking and feeling better than I had in years. I was much more confident and experiencing all the benefits of my healthy lifestyle. But for some reason I felt my motivation to continue working out starting to wane. Again I stepped back and examined my program. This time I took a good, hard look at motivation and how it works.

Motivation, simply stated, is an inner force that compels behavior. It's what gets you up in the morning. It's what excites you to action.

I had started to lose my direction. I had lost the big picture. I was no longer focusing on the ultimate me. I had become caught up in how many pounds I had lost, what percentage of body fat I had lost, what size clothes I was wearing. I had stopped striving for the ultimate me and had become focused on moving away from being fat.

When I first decided that I needed to over-haul myself, my inspiration was sparked by the desire to develop a new ultimate me. I was not motivated to exercise myself away from tight jeans or from weighing 250 lbs. There's a big difference!

A fundamental key to constructing a successful motivational program is that it be pointed in the right direction. There are two motivational directions: motivation toward and motivation away. Though both directions work as a compelling force, they are quite different.

A person who is motivated away from being out of shape will be limited to being motivated only while the jeans are tight. When the jeans fit loosely, this person's motivation will fade until it no longer exists. Many people have experienced this when they choose to lose 10 pounds before vacation. After losing the 10 pounds and achieving their goal, they stop. Some go through this cycle all their lives, resulting in feelings of total failure.

A person whose motivation moves toward a goal will stay motivated because he or she will always be striving to get there.

A person whose motivation moves toward a goal will stay motivated because he or she will always be striving to get there. For instance, if my goal is the image of the ultimate me, I will continue to stay motivated even after I have lost 10, 20 or even 30 pounds, gained strength in my legs, and/or rehabilitated an injury. My motivation will remain firm because even though I have achieved many things, my main goal—my ultimate me—still stands in front of me.

Also, being motivated to move away from fat thighs, a big bottom, or a flabby stomach leads to a negative mindset, forcing one to concentrate on what we don't want instead of what we do want. Being motivated to move toward the goal of achieving the ultimate you forces you to concentrate on what you do want.

Once you have your motivation pointed in the right direction, it is still going to take effort to keep it alive. One way to stay motivated is to place a high value on your body. Giving something value creates action. Placing value on achieving it will help you to discover how much this goal is worth to you and that will cause you to act accordingly. When we fail to live up to our values, the result is frustration and

I began to write down everything I ate and the effect of that food on my body. I kept track of what I ate, when I ate it, where I ate it, and how it made me feel.

disappointment. And disappointment is counterproductive to motivation.

Once I had my motivation straightened out, my ultimate me image was becoming sharper in my mind as I drew closer to it. I still practiced positive self-talk and I was vigilant to guard against letting self-doubt creep in. As my confidence grew, I was less sheepish about letting people know what I was trying to accomplish in my life. Before I had sort of hid it, I was embarrassed to tell people. But I was overcoming that lack of confidence. I knew I was ready to succeed when someone complimented me and I was simply able to say, "Thank you," instead of hem-hawing around or making light of my achievement. I was positive and I tried to surround myself with positive people. I also began to withdraw from people who were negative.

This leads me to an important point. I feel I must warn you that the mental aspect of Phase 2 can be very difficult in terms of relationships with other people. We say that opposites attract, but in reality we attract people who are similar to ourselves. I was changing, and the people in my circle weren't. That caused friction. I was a challenge to the status quo. When I shed my baggy clothes and began to wear more stylish clothes, I heard remarks about how I was dressing like a teenager. Family members commented that I was obsessed with working out when I was only training 4 to 5 hours a week. It wasn't the time or the clothes or the new look of my body—it was deeper than that. I felt good about myself, my career was taking off, I was jetsetting around the world on corporate jets with Tom Monaghan—everything about me was changing. I was no longer the overweight ex-jock doomed to live paycheck to paycheck on a job that didn't mean anything to me. I was becoming a new person, and that was unsettling to people who had known the old me. They weren't changing, and I was a threat.

I've seen it many times with my clients. They begin training, their confidence skyrockets, their life takes off—then their personal relationships become rocky. I've seen marriages break-up, business partnerships dissolve, friendships fizzle. My own marriage was a Phase 2 casualty. My ex-wife is one of the nicest people in the world, and she came from a solid, supportive Midwestern family, but I wasn't the same person she married.

Now, I'm not recommending that you burn all your bridges and dump everyone you know, but be prepared for some resistance. I decided to be happy with myself. Some supported that and some didn't, but I have no regrets. Now I'm happy with who I am.

My life is filled with people who accept me and support me. I have a wonderful wife, four terrific kids, two successful businesses, and I have the peace of mind that comes from putting forth my best effort in everything I do. Sure, the mental ups and downs of Phase 2 were tough, but they were a part of the journey that I wouldn't trade. If I hadn't gone through those times, I wouldn't be where I am now.

Chapter

6

advanced program

Phase 3-Advanced Level

As my body and my life changed, it became more and more clear to me that my future was in fitness. The benefits were so incredible that I wanted to tell people what I had found and how fitness could change not just their bodies, but their lives, too. Fitness was like a suit of armor that gave me the confidence and energy to take on the world. It gave me the confidence to walk away from lucrative future with Domino's Pizza and to financially start over and pursue my dream of helping others find fitness. I moved to another city and began selling fitness equipment. After I had mastered the advanced level, I had the courage to again walk away from a six-figure income and start my own business. I had conquered my own bad habits and negative thoughts—and I knew I could conquer the business world.

Physically I had plateaued at the intermediate level. But this time I knew the answer was to challenge myself. I had the enthusiasm, the passion and the desire to take my training to that level. I was ready to go farther. I also knew that there would be a cost, that the advanced level would require sacrifice. But the impact of training on my life had been so great, not just healthwise but also in my career and in my personal life, that I had to go for it. I felt that the more I pursued excellence in my own body, the more success I would experience in all areas of my life.

Training at this level isn't for everybody. It is better to maintain the beginner or intermediate levels then to burn out trying to fit the advanced level into a lifestyle that can't handle it. But the advanced level also isn't just for people in the fitness industry. It's really about personality. This step is so far beyond shaping up and looking good. It's about pursuing excellence, and it's for that type of person. From artists to bankers, men and women, regardless of race or age, the advanced level is about self-actualization, being the most true to who you are and your purpose in life. Each individual has to look at their own situation—their career, their family, the price they are willing to pay. For instance, if you have a full schedule, but you're not going to set up a good home gym, that's a huge obstacle.

Moving up to the advanced level of training excited me and it fit my personality. This is training at a very instinctual level. It's where effort becomes effortless. My self-image had changed so drastically since I had begun training. I no longer thought of myself as a struggling college drop-out. Now I was the character image I had imagined in my kitchen so long ago, I was a peak performer, and I had no doubt that I could achieve the next level.

When training at the beginning level, the idea had been to work my entire body as one muscle grouping. At the intermediate level, I added more muscle-specific exercises for definition. At the advanced level, I began working much more in-depth with muscle-specific exercises, as you will see. Each area of my body was broken down and trained as specifically as possible. I found that by doing this I was able to mold and sculpt my body the way I wished.

Now my goal was to train seven hours every seven days, allowing for at least a day of rest for the muscles worked. Here I actually cut down my aerobic training to twice a week. I found that less was more for me. This approach didn't make me gain weight or leave me winded after walking up a flight of stairs. To the contrary, I found my cardiovascular health very easy to maintain. More than twice a week was overtraining for me. Sometimes less is more. I have a family and two businesses to run. I don't want to spend more time in the gym just to spend time there. I want my body to be the best it can so I can live my life the best I can. If I can do that in seven hours a week, I say great!

I have a family and two businesses to run. I don't want to spend more time in the gym just to spend time there.

Because I had purchased good quality professional equipment during the intermediate phase, I had everything I needed to advance my program. If you want to pursue the advanced level, please take my advice and invest in your own equipment. When I bought my equipment, I couldn't really afford it, but with all that training was giving me, I didn't see how I could afford not to buy it. I was worth the investment. We think nothing of an important person such as the President having an expensive gym in the White House so that he can stay on top of his health. In fact, we want him to have it so he'll be at his best when guiding our country. Well, you are just as valuable as he is, your health is just as important. After all the changes I had experienced since I began my overhaul, I couldn't deny how entwined the body and mind were, and how much I needed the equipment. I took the plunge. Since I was selling equipment, I was lucky enough to have a discount, but I can tell you I would have paid whatever the cost. You have to find a way to do what matters most to you.

Don't expect to jump from the phase two to phase three all at once. You need to make a slow transition from one phase to the next for two reasons. First, a sudden jump in intensity may lead to injury, fatigue and burnout. Secondly, this level of training may be more than you are ready for or want. Psychologically, it may be premature to move to the next phase. Remember, this is definitely not for everyone.

I stopped eating based on hunger, and I began eating for performance.

Nutrition

In the intermediate level I became more informed about what different types of food did for my body. At the advanced level I focused on how much I needed of each type of food. During this time I perfected the ratio of carbohydrates, proteins and fats my body needed for peak performance, maximum energy and muscle development. I did this by continuing my food journal and listening to what my body was telling me. Maybe this sounds vague, but at this point I was so in tune with my body, I knew when a food brought my energy level down. I could feel when I was low on carbs.

I stopped eating based on hunger, and I began eating for performance. Back then I was working long hours. Now I drive 1000 miles a week and fly even more. I have to keep my energy levels up, and I eat accordingly. I still emphasized carbs in the morning and protein at night, but now I eat smaller meals more times throughout the day. For breakfast I'd have some slow-burning complex carbohydrates plus some simple carbohydrates for quick energy. I'd have good amount of protein, too.

During the day I would mix proteins and carbs in a morning snack, lunch, and an afternoon snack. For dinner I had little carbs, and mostly protein, and before bed I'd have something strictly protein such as a protein shake. I never missed meals, and I ate a varied diet. I also continued taking multivitamins.

During this time I began taking more protein supplements. If you've ever wandered into a health food store, you know the supplement aisle can be overwhelming. I looked for a good basic protein supplement from a reputable company. Read the label and avoid supplements that are high in carbohydrates—that means too much sugar. I also avoid any product that makes crazy claims. It's a supplement, not a magic potion. It can help you become your best, but it can't make you your best. Before you go into a store, get your goals in mind and read the product labels. And by all means ask for advice from the people who work in the stores; it's their business to know the products they sell.

As you push your body to its limits of performance, the food you ingest becomes more crucial. Think of your body as a race car. You wouldn't fill the tank of a million dollar Indy race car at the local convenience store gas station, so don't fill up your body there either. The importance of fueling your body properly includes one other condition relative to nutrition; namely, balance.

> ## My nutritional goals for the advanced level:
>
> Concentrate on providing my body with enough raw material to:
> - Supply energy
> - Build or maintain muscle mass
> - Control body fat
> - Contribute to general health and improved bodily functions
> - Stimulate the mind
> - Assist in recovery from workouts
> - Help to relieve pain, soreness, and fatigue

The Balance

For me the key to nutritional mastery was balancing the ratio between carbohydrates, proteins and fats. I needed to find the right combination for my body. Fine-tuning the ratio between these components took lots of experimentation. Being aware of the calorie content in food is important, but in solving the balance equation, I found it unnecessary to count calories.

Carbohydrates

Nutritionists can't agree on how many carbohydrates a person should consume. At the advanced level, you need to pay attention to the kind of carbohydrates you consume (simple, complex) keeping in mind that carbohydrates are your primary source of energy.

Your digestive system converts all sugar and starches into glucose—blood sugar. It then converts the glucose into muscle glycogen stored inside the muscle cells. This blood-bone glucose supplies the immediate energy needs of your brain and working muscles. If any blood glucose is left over two to three hours after you eat (there will be some left over if you overeat), the excess will be converted into adipose tissue—stored energy.

The key to calculating proper carbohydrate intake is to know the rate at which carbohydrates are converted into blood sugar and metabolized as energy. Keep in mind that complex carbohydrates—whole grains, nuts, vegetables and some fruits—are converted into blood sugar at a slow rate. That is why complex carbohydrates are the preferred fuel for sustaining energy. Their molecular structure provides long term energy. Therefore, you need to supply your body with an adequate amount of complex carbohydrates to get enough glucose and glycogen for energy.

Simple carbohydrates do not yield energy at a slow steady rate. They quickly convert into blood glucose, and that's why foods high in sugar or processed white flour will give you an initial rush of energy. Your blood sugar soars, but then you drop like a brick off a tall building as your blood sugar level plummets. This sudden drop can cause fatigue, nervousness and headaches. When these symptoms hit, you will crave sugar or processed white flour. If you succumb to these cravings, the vicious cycle will continue. It's not unlike a drug addict's situation; therefore, you must break the cycle of giving yourself a sugar "fix."

The key to calculating proper carbohydrate intake is to know the rate at which carbohydrates are converted into blood sugar and metabolized as energy.

Glycemic Index

Not all simple carbohydrates have a yo-yo effect on your blood glucose, and not all complex carbohydrates take a long time to break down into blood sugar. That's what makes separating good carbohydrates from bad ones so difficult. Luckily, scientists have done the work for us by charting carbohydrate foods on a glycemic index based on blood glucose response.

For example, apples, oranges, whole wheat, oats and brown rice have relatively slow burning rates making these foods good energy sources. Caution though. When using the glycemic index to choose your energy sources, keep in mind that just because something has a low glycemic index doesn't mean you can overindulge in it. Choose foods with a good to moderate glycemic index rating and examine the ingredients to make sure that they fit your goals of eating low fat, low sugar and low sodium. Choose to ingest low glycemic rated food for long term energy—before exercising—mid-glycemic rated food for mid-range energy, and a few of the higher glycemic index foods for quick energy. Eating too many higher glycemic index foods will cause your blood sugar levels/energy to yo-yo. So be careful. Remember that balance is the key.

There is no simple answer to the question "how much or what percentage of carbohydrates should I follow?" You will need to experiment and find out what ratio is best for your system. A few issues are apparent, however. Complex carbohydrates should make up a majority of your carbohydrate intake. Most simple carbohydrates are low in vitamins and minerals—an overconsumption of simple carbohydrates will generally cause indigestion, heartburn, nausea and excess body fat.

Some of the glycemic index ratings may surprise you. White potatoes, bananas, and white rice have high glycemic index values which means that they cause a rapid rise and fall in blood sugar levels. Even though these are healthy foods, you should not overindulge in them. Nutritional experts recommend consuming foods that are in the 40 to 80 percent range on the index. My experience has been that sticking with foods in the 40 to 50 percent range work best. I eat mostly complex carbohydrates—bread, oats, peas—and a few simple carbohydrates—apples, bananas, fruit cookies. I have learned that I need to eat carbohydrates early in the day for energy. In fact, recently I have found that by watching my consumption of carbohydrates after six o'clock in the evening has helped me become much more lean.

> In fact, recently I have found that by watching my consumption of carbohydrates after six o'clock in the evening has helped me become much more lean.

Protein

How much protein does your body need? Neither the experts nor I can tell you how much protein is enough for you. Only you can decide by reading your body's signals. I can give you basic information that will help you after you have received these natural signals. The general rule for a training athlete is: one half to one gram of protein per pound of body weight. You can compute this figure by dividing the total number of calories by total number of protein grams. The government disagrees with this amount but many professional athletes with really fit bodies criticize the government's recommendations.

Too much protein consumption can cause as much damage as too little. An overconsumption of protein can cause urea (the formation of highly toxic ammonia). Urea must be excreted from the body and this elimination process puts a strain on the liver and kidneys.

Stick with protein sources that provide a complete amino acid profile. Lean red meats, chicken, fish and poultry are the best sources. I supplement my diet with protein in shake form. Some people report that they do better with one source of protein over another. My wife does very well with chicken, fish and turkey, but does not like how she feels after eating red meat. Her body sends her signals of discomfort to let her know that red meat doesn't agree with her system. By carefully monitoring your body's signals, you too will be able to establish the best protein sources for your system.

Fats

It should be apparent that humans cannot be totally fat-free as some national advertisers would like us to believe. Our bodies need fats as a secondary source of energy when muscle glycogen stores are depleted. The hardest question to answer is how much fat does your body need to function properly? The Recommended Daily Allowance (RDA) is 30 percent. However, as an example, my body responds best when I keep my fat intake down to 10 to 20 percent. This ratio provides my system with enough fat for bodily functions while satisfying my hunger. Dry scalp, irritability, dry skin, and an inability to satisfy hunger are the signals my body sends when I am not consuming enough fat. When this happens I increase my fat intake by ingesting some oil or natural peanut butter.

Its a good idea to consume unsaturated fats. They are necessary for normal growth, healthy blood, arteries and nerves, and they help to transport and break down cholesterol. The best sources of unsaturated fats are: polyunsaturated—safflower, sunflower and corn oils—and monounsaturated—peanut, olive and avocado oils. Avoid saturated fats (butter, lard, etc.). They are derived mainly from animal sources and are easy to recognize because they harden at room temperature.

The demands of advanced level training may at times cause your system to require more fat. Watch for the signals I mentioned above, and when you experience the symptoms, increase your fat intake for a couple of meals. You'll see and feel a positive response. The most important thing to remember regarding

> By carefully monitoring your body's signals, you to will be able to establish the best protein sources for your system.

fat consumption is to not eliminate all fat from your diet. Just keep fat consumption under control. Consuming too little fat may inhibit the body's ability to metabolize existing body fat. This slowing process may cause the body to hoard body fat. So, experiment with different amounts until your body tells you how much fat you need to consume.

Vitamins and Minerals

If you are confused about vitamins and minerals, you are in good company. I have been bumping my head against the vitamin and mineral confusion wall for years. However, I am certain of one thing. Despite what some experts say, consuming vitamins and minerals is very important.

Many nutritionists believe that supplementation is not necessary for good health. They claim that eating a balanced diet will supply the body with all of the vitamins and minerals it needs. But most people don't eat balanced diets. And too much of what we eat comes from processed, overcooked or empty calorie foods. Therefore, I think vitamin and mineral supplementation is vital for developing a healthy body.

Vitamins and minerals do not supply energy directly, but they are essential for the regulation of the biochemical process in which protein, carbohydrates and fats are broken down to yield energy.

Vitamins are organic substances which help form bones and tissues. Vitamins regulate our metabolism by assisting the enzymes to carry out various functions, such as converting carbohydrates and fats into energy. Vitamins are found in minute quantities (milligrams and micrograms) in food and are also available in supplemental form as capsules, powders and tablets.

The two categories of vitamins are water-soluble and fat-soluble. Water-soluble vitamins are not stored in the body, and any excess is flushed out in the urine. Fat-soluble vitamins are dissolved and stored in the fatty tissues of the body. Though it is necessary to take water-soluble vitamins daily, you may ingest fat-soluble vitamins less frequently. As with every nutrition issue, you and you alone must determine how much supplementation your body requires. You must experiment to find the right balance for your body.

Vitamin C (ascorbic acid) is one of the most important of all the vitamins. Without enough vitamin C, you get tired rapidly, recover from injuries slowly, and fall victim to severe stress. Scurvy, a potentially fatal disease, with symptoms such as bleeding gums and extreme weakness, is a severe reaction to Vitamin C deficiency.

Ascorbic acid helps you get the most out of your muscles in a variety of ways. It aids muscle tissue in utilizing fatty acids as an energy source, thereby conserving glycogen, the major fuel, and adding endurance. Vitamin C helps your body use iron and oxygen efficiently while protecting other vitamins from harmful oxygenation. Recent research also indicates that Vitamin C slows down lactic acid buildup during exertion, thereby minimizing fatigue. Also, like B6, Vitamin C protects your body against the harmful effects of stress by keeping the adrenal glands working.

Vitamin C's primary role is as a biochemical partner in the formation and maintenance of collagen, the protein "cement" that binds connective tissue. Collagen holds together muscles, skin, bones and organs—literally your whole body. Though many believe that oranges are the best source for Vitamin C, they are not. Some oranges have plenty of ascorbic acid, while others have only trace levels. Eating a dozen oranges a day can't guarantee that you'll get your daily require-ment. Supplementation is the solution.

Vitamin E is the name given to a number of related viscous oils that work to keep the cardiovascular system clear and dilated, thus increasing the blood supply to your extremities. This nutrient also protects muscle and nerve tissue from overoxygenation while, at the same time, enabling your muscles to get by on less oxygen. In simple terms: Vitamin E promotes endurance.

Vitamin C (ascorbic acid) is one of the most important of all the vitamins.

The only way to ensure that you are getting the nutrients you need is to take supplements every day. Though the supplement market is enormous and can be intimidating and confusing, to determine what dosage you need, purchase one of the multi-mineral packs. Almost all of the major vitamin manufacturers provide all the vitamins and minerals you need in one small cellophane package. By using the multi pack, you don't have to open dozens of bottles every morning. This is the most convenient way to take vitamin and mineral supplements.

Be warned, however! Saturating your system with vitamins will not cause miracles to happen and may even be toxic. The real value of vitamin/mineral supplements comes from taking them on a daily basis for several months. Following this routine will help you see and feel the difference.

Also, remember that intense training robs the body of fluids, so make sure you drink plenty of water.

Motivation

Understanding motivation is the key to developing it. All motivation come from two areas of the mind — memory and imagination. The two types of motivation are: intrinsic (inner feelings, labor of love) and extrinsic (payoff, paycheck, good grades, losing weight for a bet). Extrinsic motivation will not help you to maintain your body once you have met your goal. However, intrinsic motivation will. It is best because it is stimulated internally. Intrinsic motivation will propel you to the top of your achievement level and help keep you there.

To increase your intrinsic motivation, you must work to build internal standards. You must explore, be curious, and stop focusing on the payoffs and rewards. You should stimulate your imagination with positive feelings about what you are trying to achieve. The kind of motivation that will sustain you for a lifetime must come from within, and it is never too late to develop your imagination to help provide this kind of motivation. Simply take the lid off your creativity. Allow your senses the freedom to explore, relearn what living really feels like, and you will become inspired to feel your motivation from within. Motivation is a fire that you light from within—imagination is the spark that lights the flame.

To increase your intrinsic motivation, you must work to build internal standards.

I began this level knowing that I had to be willing to allot the necessary hours, energy and effort to reach my full potential. In order to move into this phase successfully, I had to first redefine my direction. My body and mindset had changed since the first and second phase training levels. Advancing my training to a higher level of excellence meant learning how to get the most out of myself. I worked to bring my mind, and body into harmony.

The desire to go beyond your current level of existence, the hunger to push your limits and climb to the peak of excellence, has no end. The destination will always be the endless horizon. I could only reach excellence by making demands on myself and working to meet those demands. In pursuing potential, I had to step out of the arena of "what is" into the arena of "what could be." In this phase of my training program, I viewed each training session as a reenactment of life's struggles. The goal was to achieve something greater than I achieved the day before.

Achieving excellence in anything depends largely on three basic factors: how well you know where you want to go, how determined you are to get there, and how strongly you believe in your ability to arrive at your desired destination. In pursuing excellence, I focused energy on those aspects of performance that were within my control—developing skills, preparation, execution, doing the best I could do that day.

Contentment with the status quo always leads to a lack of effort, which leads to an unfulfilled life and unhappiness. Happiness is connected to action. Action that leads to the fulfillment of a goal requires commitment, integrity, motivation and ambition. This was the cornerstone that I built my program on.

Your performance is determined by your expectations for yourself. If you treat yourself as if you have something to offer, as if you have a lot of potential, then you will behave accordingly. If you treat yourself as if you have little or nothing to offer, then that will likewise be reflected in your performance. So don't sell yourself short. You are only as good as the expectations you have for yourself. In order to reach your goals, you must believe, and you must expect to succeed.

Too often, after experiencing a few setbacks, some people convince themselves that they will continue to fail. These people begin expecting failure; consequently, they achieve it. This negative expectation is called learned helplessness. It is a false belief that you are at the mercy of external forces—a job, other people, metabolism or "things"—that are causing you to fail. It is a totally destructive mindset that you must discard. However, the ironic thing about failure is that the more you do it, the more you learn how to avoid it, and the more likely success becomes.

The greatest barriers we run up against in anything are always psychological—the mental barriers we place in front of us. To reach my potential I had to be committed and constantly stretch what I perceive to be my limits. To become my best, I had to become supercharged and superfocused. It takes an incredible amount of commitment to reach this level of development—the commitment to train and rest your body so that you can perform, and the commitment to train your mind to focus precisely on what you are doing and what you want to achieve.

Wanting to rebuild my body to this level meant that I had to be totally committed to doing so. A commitment to do the work is a prerequisite for all excellence, but unless you also master the art of self-control, you will not reach your goal. Excellence requires the development of good focusing skills, as well as an openness to learning. I had a choice to make: I could either stay where I was, or I could choose to pursue excellence. It was

Your performance is determined by your expectations for yourself.

important to recognize that I did have a choice. Having the ability to choose, having control over my situation, allowed me to approach the situation more positively. By making the choice and taking control, I had a greater capacity to endure the demands that I encountered. You must make a conscious decision.

The Phase Three- Advanced Level Program

The results I received from the first two phases of my training program were very satisfying. I would say 95% of the people I have consulted are content to continue with the phase two program, and that's great. I, however, wanted to push the envelope.

At some point the advice, coaching, instruction that others give you can only take you so far. There comes a point when you simply have to take the reins and guide yourself because ultimately you are your best coach. Success at phase three requires that your training become instinctual. You have to become in tune to the body's signals—a master at prescribing exactly what your body needs to get to and maintain this level of excellence.

Instinctive training required that I learn to read my body's signals, analyze the information, and react with the right action. This required

Contentment with the status quo always leads to a lack of effort, which leads to an unfulfilled life and unhappiness.

that I develop a connection between the subtle signals my body sent and the rate of results I achieved through training. Reacting appropriately to this feedback, by altering my program accordingly until it approached the ideal formula, was the secret. Developing an intuitive feel, an internal guidance, that told me when to train, what to train, how much to train, when to rest, when to eat, what to eat, etc. Reaching this level of mastery required several years of experimentation, but once I found the success formula, I had perfect control of my body.

Another lesson I learned in this level was to practice intelligent training—making the most gains from the least amount of training. The "more is better" or "no pain, no gain" approach doesn't work. It always causes imbalance and leads to overtraining, injury and burnout. My goal was to make my workout efficient and sensible thus promoting longevity.

Although the routine I had followed up until this point had worked well for initial results, the desire to improve on what I had accomplished forced me to rethink my routine. Because of my schedule I would have to get into the gym almost every day. My workouts would have to be focused, and I would have to be able to complete them in around 60 minutes. I decided what was going to work best for me at this point was a floating training schedule.

Day one — chest, calves, lower back, abs
Day two — shoulders, triceps, abs,
Day three — 40 min jog or stationary bike
Day four — legs, abs
Day five — back, biceps, forearms, abs
Day six — 40 min jog or stationary bike
Day seven — start the sequence again

The basic structure of my program was slightly changed as I no longer did aerobic exercise after weight training. I began each workout slowly with a 10-minute aerobic warm-up riding my stationary bike at an easy pace. Once I had warmed up, I moved through the weight training part of the workout then cooled down with stretches. Two workouts a week were strictly aerobic with stretching.

You have to become in tune to the body's signals—a master at prescribing exactly what your body needs to get to and maintain this level of excellence.

The Many Benefits Stretching

One of the big changes made in this phase was implementing more stretching. I began stretching each muscle I worked after the completion of each set. Not only did this help me with my flexibility and prevent injuries, but it greatly enhanced my overall development and muscle appearance. What few people realize about stretching is that it is a great way to define and shape the body. Stretching also helps teach you to isolate the muscle or muscle group you are targeting by enhancing the muscle pump. That is important because the pump tells you that you worked the muscle sufficiently.

Another great bonus to stretching in between sets is that it helps pace the workout. You perform a set, stretch, change weight and then immediately start the next set. This helps keep your focus through your routine.

In order to properly stretch a muscle, you must ease into the stretch slowly. Continue the stretch to the point just before you sense pain or when you begin to feel a slight pain in the muscle being stretched. Once you reach this point, hold the stretch without bouncing for 10 to 15 seconds, then slowly ease out of the stretch.

Symmetry refers to the balance between the left and right side of the body. Proportion refers to the overall relationship between the size and degree of development of all body parts. Muscular definition refers to the degree of development in a muscle and can be enhanced by using advanced training techniques cutting down on rest time between sets, adding additional cardiovascular training sessions, and, most importantly, following good solid nutritional practices.

Another great bonus to stretching in between sets is that it helps pace the workout.

Size/mass refers to how big a muscle is. You can best accomplish appropriate muscle size by lifting heavy weights in a controlled manner with emphasis on the negative portion of the lift.

Shape, the pattern in the lines of a muscle and quality of the muscle mass, gives the body a pleasing appearance. Seeing big numbers on a tape measure, striving for the "I can kick sand in your face" look, and not paying attention to overall body symmetry and body fat, will only make the body appear swollen, stuffed and out of balance. Remember, the truly beautiful physique presents a balanced appearance.

With a well-proportioned, balanced body, you can achieve enhanced athletic performance. For example, many golfers try to strengthen just their forearm muscles thinking that will improve their golf swings. What they need to do is develop all of their muscles, especially their lower back and abdominal muscles which play a more crucial role in swinging a golf club. Again, the key is balance. The perfect classic look is measured by good development of the calves, abdominals and shoulders/deltoids.

CHEST

1. Inner Chest: Close Grip Smith Machine Press

I performed 3 sets increasing the weight 5-10 lbs each set. The first set I used a weight that allowed me to perform around 12 reps. The second set I performed 10 reps, and the third set I performed 6-8 reps. I stretched the muscles after each set using the chest stretch.

DAY 1
ROUTINE

CHEST,
CALVES,
LOWER BACK,
ABS

2. Upper Pectoral: Incline Dumbbell Press

I performed 3 sets increasing the weight 5-10 lbs each set. The first set I used a weight that allowed me to perform around 12 reps. The second set I performed 10 reps, and the third set I performed 6-8 reps. I stretched the muscles after each set using the chest stretch.

The Chest

My goal was to use a combination of exercises that emphasized each area of the chest, striving for a balanced, proportionate, symmetrical, well-defined chest. To fully develop and complete the chest, I focused on individual exercises that emphasized each of the key areas, the inside, outside, upper and lower areas of the chest muscle.

The two basic exercises for the chest are presses (you press the weight away from the chest) and flys (you draw your extended arms together across the chest in a hugging motion). The chest exercises I have listed helped me achieve complete chest development.

DAY 1 ROUTINE

3. Lower Pectorals: Decline Dumbbell Press

I performed 3 sets increasing the weight 5-10 lbs each set.
The first set I used a weight that allowed me to perform around 12 reps.
The second set I performed 10 reps, and the third set I performed
6-8 reps. I stretched the muscles after each set using the chest stretch.

begin
finish
stretch

1   2   3

4. Outer Chest: Dumbbell Incline Flys

I performed 3 sets increasing the weight 5-10 lbs each set. The
first set I used a weight that allowed me to perform around 12 reps.
The second set I performed 10 reps, and the third set I performed
6-8 reps. I stretched the muscles after each set using the chest stretch.

begin
finish
stretch

1   2   3

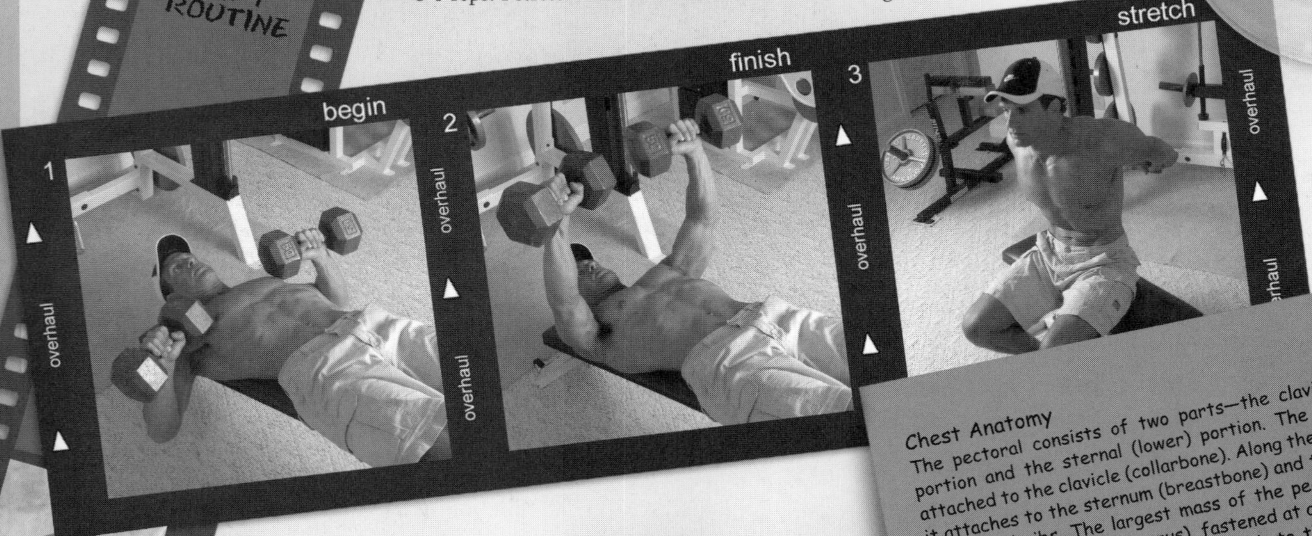

Chest Anatomy
The pectoral consists of two parts—the clavicular (upper) portion and the sternal (lower) portion. The upper part is attached to the clavicle (collarbone). Along the mid-body line, it attaches to the sternum (breastbone) and to the cartilage of several ribs. The largest mass of the pectoral starts at the upper arm bone (humerus), fastened at a point under and just above where the deltoids attach to the humerus. The pectorals spread out like a fan and cover the rib cage like armor plates. Attached to the rib cage in the center and across to the shoulder, this muscle lets you perform such motions as pitching a ball underhanded, doing a wide arm bench press, or twisting a cap off a bottle.

DAY 1
ROUTINE

CHEST,
CALVES,
LOWER BACK,
ABS

CALVES

1. Inside of Calves: Standing Calf Raises (Toes Pointed Out)
I performed two sets increasing the weight 20 lbs each set.
I kept my reps in the 12-15 rep range.

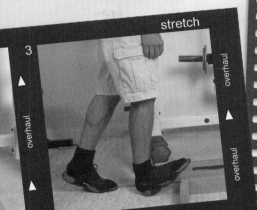

2. Outside of Calves: Standing Calf Raises (Toes Pointed In)
I performed two sets increasing the weight 20 lbs each set.
I kept my reps in the 12-15 rep range.

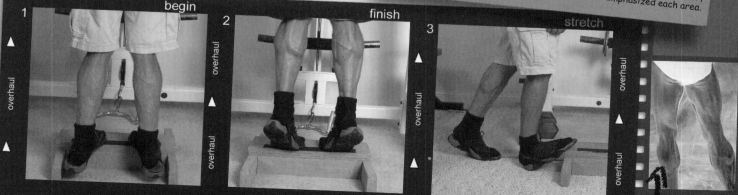

The Calves

A good pair of calves look great on both men and women, but calves are considered to be one of the most difficult muscle groups to develop. They get tremendous use when you walk or run, turn, twist and raise up. To perform any of these movements, the calf muscles must bear all of the body's weight. Therefore, in order for the calves to respond to exercise, you must use several specialized movements.

The primary exercise for the calves is the standing calf raise. This exercise works both the gastrocnemius and the soleus. The calves are tough and accustomed to great amount of stress, so the best way to get a response from them is to subject them to a variety of exercise movements.

I found it best to divide the calves into four different areas: lower, upper, inner and outer. I choose exercises that emphasized each area.

109

DAY I
ROUTINE

3. Upper Calves: Standing Calf Raises
I performed three sets increasing the weight 20 lbs each set.
I kept my reps in the 12-15 rep range.

4. Lower Calves: Seated Calf Raise
I performed three sets increasing the weight 10 lbs each set.
I kept my reps in the 12-15 rep range.

Calf Anatomy
The primary muscles of the calf are the soleus, gastrocnemius and the tibialis anterior. The soleus is the larger and deeper of the calf muscles and originates from both the fibula and the tibia. Its basic function is to flex the foot. The gastrocnemius has two heads, one originating from the lateral aspect and the other from the medial of the lower femur. Both heads join to overlay the soleus and join with and insert into the Achilles tendon which inserts into the heel bone. The basic function of the gastrocnemius is to flex the foot. The tibialis anterior runs up the front of the lower leg alongside the shinbone. Its basic function is to flex the foot.

DAY 1
ROUTINE

CHEST,
CALVES,
LOWER BACK,
ABS

ABS
1. Upper Abs: Crunches (Feet on Bench)
I performed three sets of 12-15 reps.

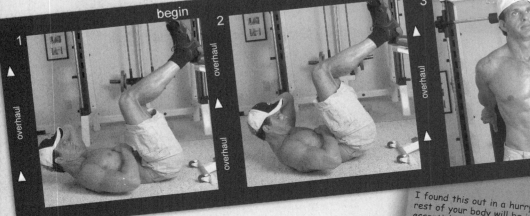

2. Lower Abs: Hanging Leg Raises
I performed three sets of 12-15 reps.

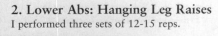

The Abdominals

I found this out in a hurry: If your abdomen is in terrific shape, the rest of your body will be in terrific shape, too. Strong abdominals are essential in achieving maximum performance in almost all sports. To better my abdominal development, I divided the abdomen into four separate areas: the upper and lower abs, and the obliques and intercostals. By working on the abdominals in this way, I could train each area as though it was an individual body part, thus getting the best results.

How you train your abs depends mostly on your body type. If you train the abdominal muscles with heavy weight, the muscles will become bigger and thicker. Many people actually overdevelop their abs causing them to bulge out like an inner tube around the midsection. People with small, narrow waists can enjoy success by adding weight; however, people with medium to large waists are better off not adding weight. The good thing about abs is that You can work these muscles often without becoming overtrained.

DAY 1
ROUTINE

3. Intercostals: Incline Seated Twists
I performed three sets of 12-15 reps.

Abdominal Anatomy

The abdomen, the visual center of the body, is composed of the rectus abdominis, the external obliques and the intercostals. The abdominals have a relatively simple function. They pull your upper body (rib cage) and lower body (pelvis) toward each other, and they contribute to keeping your internal organs in place.

The rectus abdominis is a long muscle extending along the length of the ventral aspect of the abdomen. This muscle originates in the area of the pubis and inserts into the cartilage of the fifth, sixth and seventh ribs. The basic function of the rectus abdominis is to flex the spinal column and draw the sternum toward the pelvis.

The external obliques (obliquus externus abdominis) are the muscles at each side of the torso (commonly referred to as the "love handles"). They are attached to the lower eight ribs and insert at the sides of the pelvis. The basic function of the external obliques is to flex and rotate the spinal column.

The intercostals are two thin planes of muscular and tendon fiber occupying the spaces between the ribs. The intercostals lift the ribs and draw them together.

4. Obliques: Seated Broomstick Twists
I performed one set of 100 reps.

LOWER BACK
Low Pulley Lower Back Extension
I performed three sets increasing the weight 10 lbs each set.
I kept my reps in the 12-15 rep range.

DAY 1
ROUTINE

CHEST,
CALVES,
LOWER BACK,
ABS

DAY 2 ROUTINE

SHOULDERS
1. Overall Shoulder Developement: Barbell Shoulder Press
I performed 3 sets increasing the weight 5-10 lbs each set. The first set I used a weight that allowed me to perform around 12 reps. The second set I performed 10 reps, and the third set I performed 6-8 reps. I stretched the muscles after each set using the shoulder stretch.

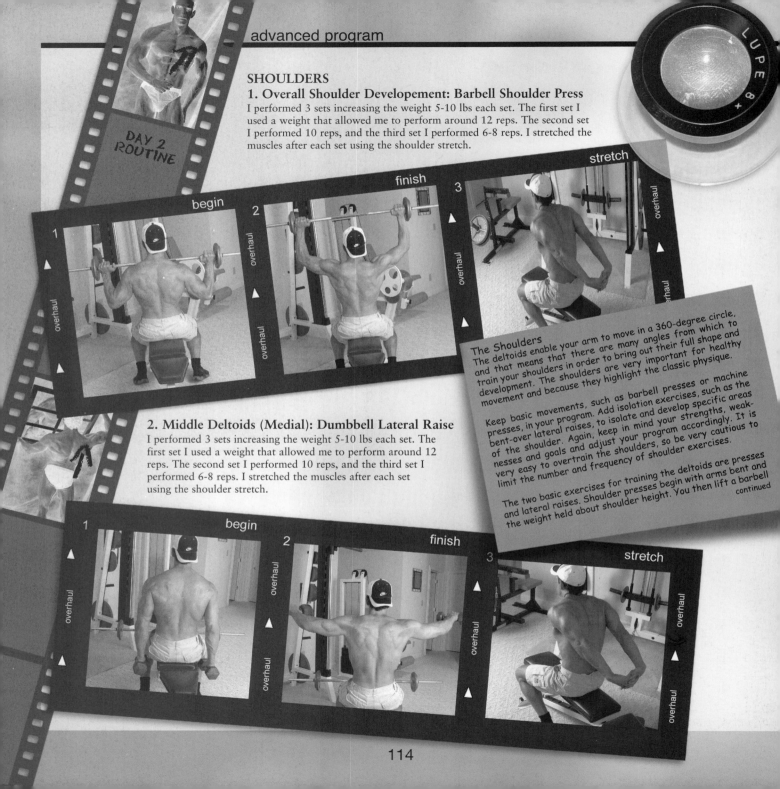

begin   finish   stretch
1   2   3

2. Middle Deltoids (Medial): Dumbbell Lateral Raise
I performed 3 sets increasing the weight 5-10 lbs each set. The first set I used a weight that allowed me to perform around 12 reps. The second set I performed 10 reps, and the third set I performed 6-8 reps. I stretched the muscles after each set using the shoulder stretch.

begin   finish   stretch
1   2   3

The Shoulders
The deltoids enable your arm to move in a 360-degree circle, and that means that there are many angles from which to train your shoulders in order to bring out their full shape and development. The shoulders are very important for healthy movement and because they highlight the classic physique.

Keep basic movements, such as barbell presses or machine presses, in your program. Add isolation exercises, such as the bent-over lateral raises, to isolate and develop specific areas of the shoulder. Again, keep in mind your strengths, weaknesses and goals and adjust your program accordingly. It is very easy to overtrain the shoulders, so be very cautious to limit the number and frequency of shoulder exercises.

The two basic exercises for training the deltoids are presses and lateral raises. Shoulder presses begin with arms bent and the weight held about shoulder height. You then lift a barbell

continued

3. Rear Deltoids (Posterior): Dumbell Bent-over Lateral Raise

I performed 3 sets increasing the weight 5-10 lbs each set. The first set I used a weight that allowed me to perform around 12 reps. The second set I performed 10 reps, and the third set I performed 6-8 reps. I stretched the muscles after each set using the shoulder stretch.

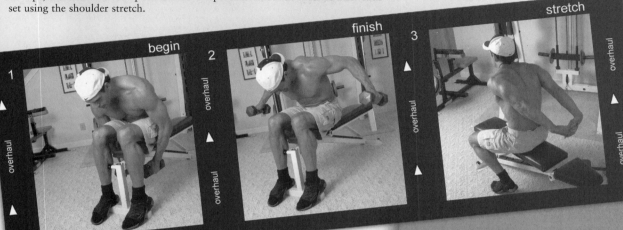

4. Front Deltoids (Anterior): Dumbbell Front Raise

I performed 3 sets increasing the weight 5-10 lbs each set. The first set I used a weight that allowed me to perform around 12 reps. The second set I performed 10 reps, and the third set I performed 6-8 reps. I stretched the muscles after each set using the shoulder stretch.

or dumbbells straight overhead. You may also perform this exercise on a machine. You can direct the stress to different deltoid heads by doing different kinds of presses—to the front or back.

Laterals involve lifting your extended arm upward in a wide arc. In order to work all three heads, you need to do laterals to the front, to the side and to the rear. When you do laterals, you completely isolate the various heads of the deltoids.

Shoulder Anatomy

The deltoids are versatile muscles that move the arm forward, backward, to the side, up and around. The deltoids have three distinct lobes of muscle called "heads" that enable this movement: the anterior head (the muscle in the front), the medial head (the muscle on the side), and the posterior head (the muscle in the rear).

DAY 2 ROUTINE

TRICEPS
1. Upper Triceps: Cable Pressdowns

I performed 3 sets increasing the weight 5-10 lbs each set. The first set I used a weight that allowed me to perform around 12 reps. The second set I performed 10 reps, and the third set I performed 6-8 reps. I stretched the muscles after each set using the triceps stretch.

begin
1

finish
2

3
stretch

2. Inner Triceps: Bench Dip

I performed 3 sets 15-20 reps. I stretched the muscles after each set using the triceps stretch.

begin
1

finish
2

3
stretch

The Triceps

The best two ways to work the triceps muscles are with pressing movements and extension movements. Even though the triceps are involved in a wide range of exercises, it is necessary, especially as you become more advanced, to isolate and stress them individually to make certain you get full development of the muscle structure. I found it best to divide the tricep muscle into three parts choosing an exercise that stressed the upper, lower and inner parts of the muscle group.

3. Lower Triceps: Dumbbell Kickback

I performed 3 sets increasing the weight 5-10 lbs each set. The first set I used a weight that allowed me to perform around 12 reps. The second set I performed 10 reps, and the third set I performed 6-8 reps. I stretched the muscles after each set using the triceps stretch.

Triceps Anatomy
The triceps (triceps brachii), a three-headed muscle that attaches under the deltoid and below the elbow, works in opposition to the biceps to straighten the arm and supinate the wrist. The triceps are larger than the biceps and make up about three-quarters of the upper arm.

ABDOMEN
1. Upper Abs: Crunch (Partial Incline Sit-up)

I performed 3 sets of 12-15 reps.

DAY 2 ROUTINE

2. Lower Abs: Seated Incline Leg Raise
I performed 3 sets of 12-15 reps.

begin 1

finish 2

stretch 3

3. Intercostals: Incline Crunch
I performed 3 sets of 12-15 reps.

begin 1

finish 2

stretch 3

4. Obliques: Hanging Side Leg Raise
I performed 1 set of 100 reps.

DAY 2
ROUTINE

SHOULDERS,
TRICEPS,
ABS

DAY 3
ROUTINE

CARDIO DAY
RIDE STATIONARY BIKE
FOR 30 MINUTES

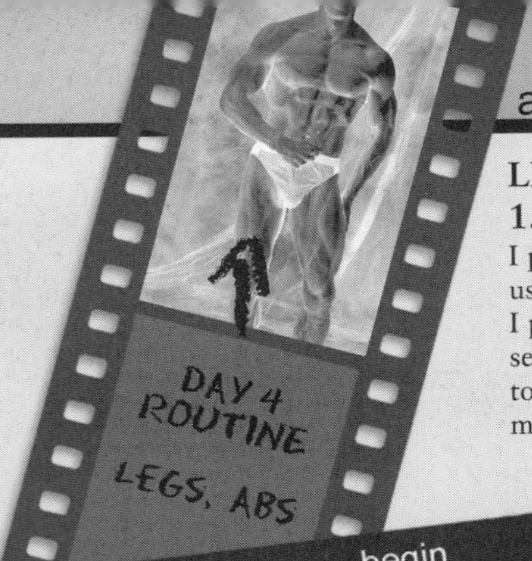

DAY 4
ROUTINE
LEGS, ABS

LEGS
1. Overall Leg: Leg Press

I performed 6 sets increasing the weight 25-30 lbs each set. The first set I used a weight that allowed me to perform around 15 reps. The second set I performed 12 reps; the third set, 10 reps; the fourth set, 6 reps; the fifth set, 4 reps. For the sixth set I did a drop set—dropping the weight down to the starting weight—and performed 20 reps. Afterward I stretched the muscle with the quadriceps stretch.

2. Quadriceps: Leg Extentsion

I performed 6 sets increasing the weight 25-30 lbs each set. The first set I used a weight that allowed me to perform around 15 reps. The second set I performed 12 reps; the third set, 10 reps; the fourth set, 6 reps; the fifth set, 4 reps. For the sixth set I did a drop set—dropping the weight down to the starting weight—and performed 20 reps. Afterward I stretched the muscle with the quadriceps stretch.

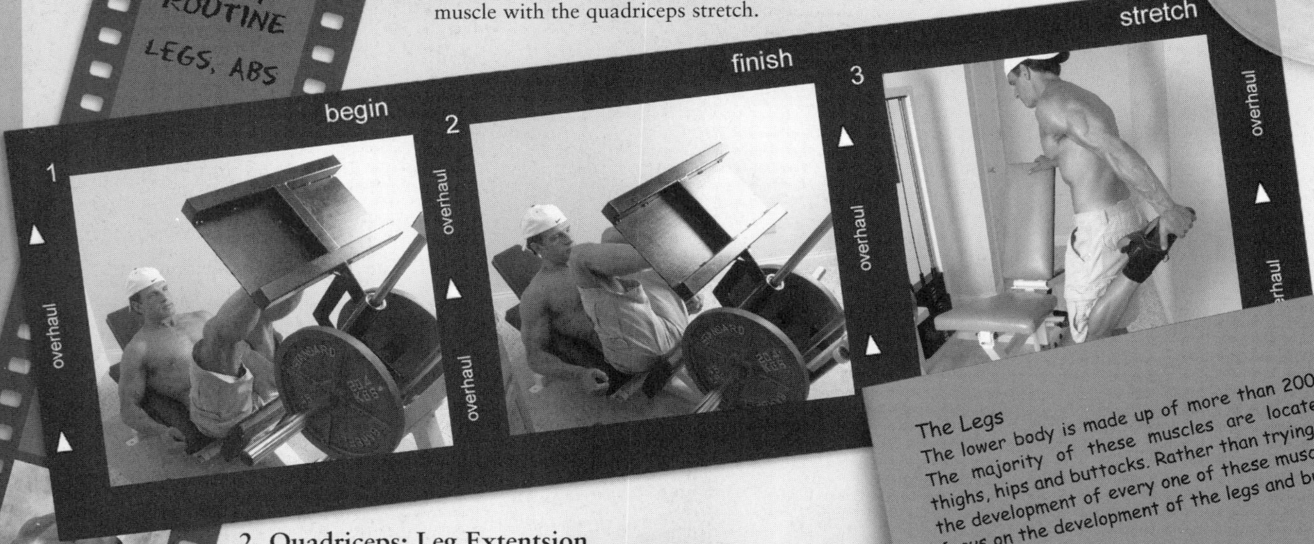

The Legs
The lower body is made up of more than 200 muscles. The majority of these muscles are located in the thighs, hips and buttocks. Rather than trying to explain the development of every one of these muscles, we will focus on the development of the legs and buttocks.

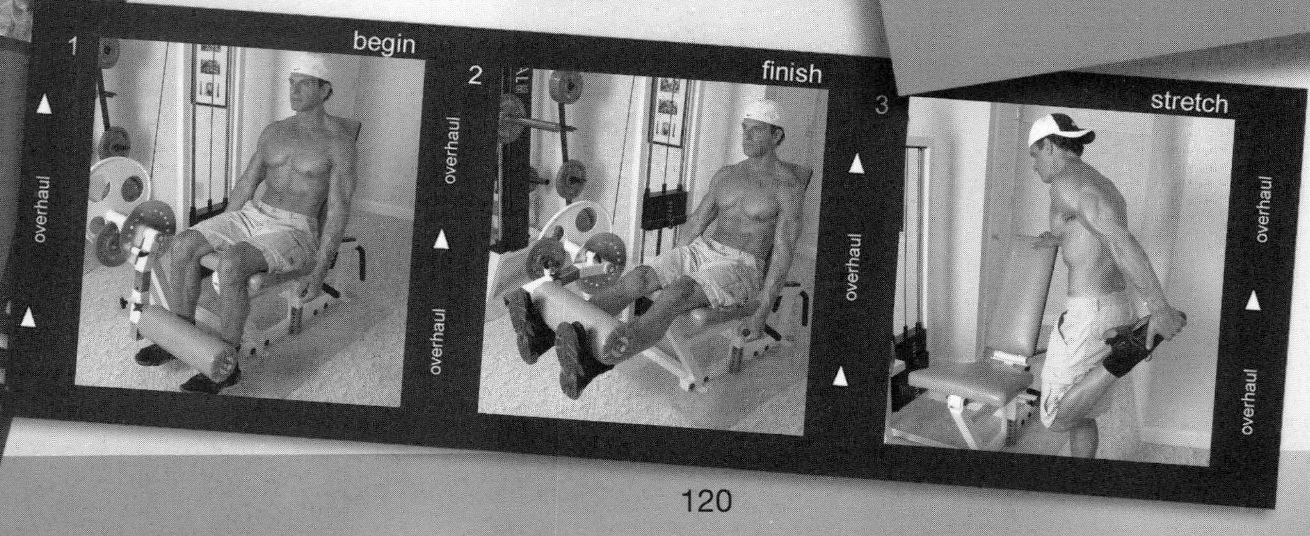

3. Quadriceps: Partial Movement Leg Extension

I performed 3 sets increasing the weight 5-10 lbs each set. The first set I used a weight that allowed me to perform around 12 reps. The second set I performed 10 reps, and the third set I performed 8 reps.

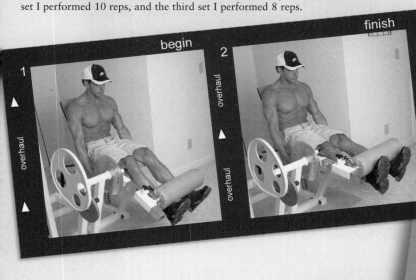

Leg Anatomy

The thigh muscles are among the largest in the human body. The main thigh muscles are the quadriceps and the hamstrings. The quads consist of four moderately large muscles that contract to straighten the leg from a fully or partially bent position. The quadriceps are composed of four muscles at the front of the thigh—rectus femoris, vastus intermedius, vastus medialis and vastus lateralis.

The primary muscle group at the back of the thigh, the hamstring, is the biceps femoris, often called the leg biceps. This muscle group contracts to bend the leg fully from a straight or partially bent position.

4. Hamstrings: Lying Leg Curls

I performed 3 sets increasing the weight 5-10 lbs each set. The first set I used a weight that allowed me to perform around 12 reps. The second set I performed 10 reps, and the third set I performed 6-8 reps. I stretched the muscles after each set using the hamstring stretch.

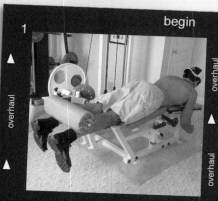

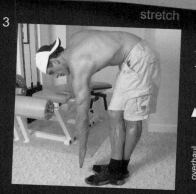
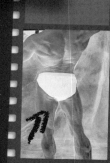

DAY 4
ROUTINE

LEGS, ABS

5. Hamstrings: Dumbbell Stiff Leg Deadlifts

I performed 3 sets increasing the weight 5-10 lbs each set. The first set I used a weight that allowed me to perform around 12 reps. The second set I performed 10 reps, and the third set I performed 6-8 reps. I stretched the muscles after each set using the glute and hamstring stretch.

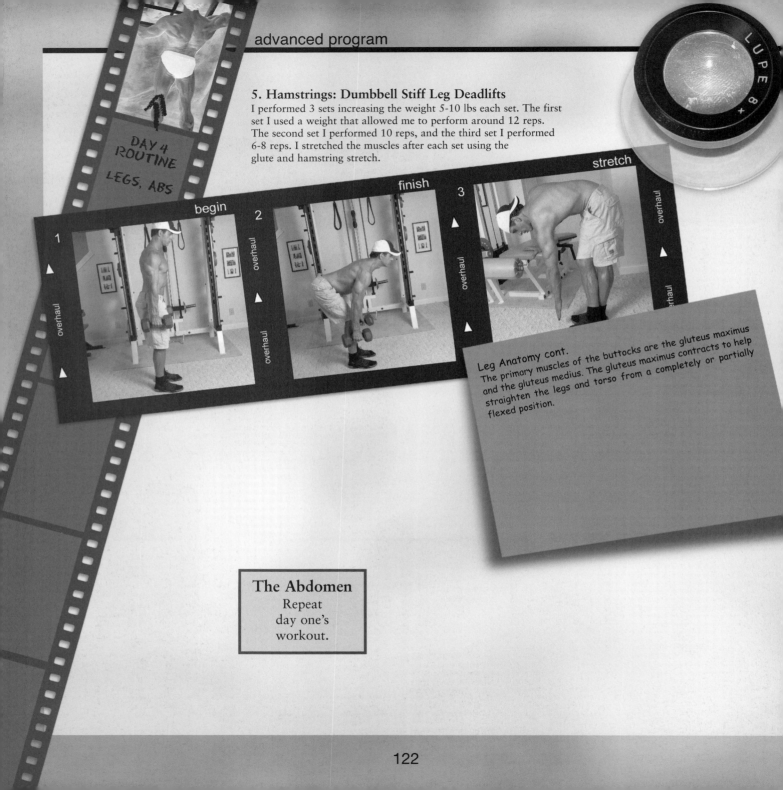

begin

finish

stretch

1

2

3

overhaul

Leg Anatomy cont.

The primary muscles of the buttocks are the gluteus maximus and the gluteus medius. The gluteus maximus contracts to help straighten the legs and torso from a completely or partially flexed position.

The Abdomen
Repeat
day one's
workout.

DAY 5
ROUTINE

BACK,
BICEPS,
FOREARM,
ABS

1. Lat Width: Front of the Neck Wide Grip Pulldown

I performed 3 sets increasing the weight 5-10 lbs each set. First set I used a weight that allowed me to perform around 12 reps. Second set 10 reps and third set 6-8 reps. I stretched the mucles after each set using the back stretch.

The Back

To completely develop the back, you need to consider how each of the important back muscles function so that you include exercises that work all the vital areas.

I found the key to effective back training is to divide the back into six areas and target each area with a specific exercise that emphasizes that area. The back consists of a number of complex and interrelated muscles that do not develop at the same rate; therefore, you should design your program to meet the needs of each of these six areas according to your strengths, weaknesses and goals.

2. Lower Lat: Close Grip Pulldowns

I performed three sets increasing the weight 5-10 lbs each set. The first set I used a weight that allowed me to perform around 12 reps. The second set I performed 10 reps, and the third set I performed 6-8 reps. I stretched the muscles after each set using the back stretch.

DAY 5 ROUTINE

3. Outer Back: One Arm Dumbbell Row

I performed three sets increasing the weight 5-10 lbs each set. The first set I used a weight that allowed me to perform around 12 reps. The second set I performed 10 reps, and the third set I performed 6-8 reps. I stretched the muscles after each set using the back stretch.

begin

1

2

finish

3

stretch

Back Anatomy

The flat triangular muscle that extends out and down from the neck and down between the shoulder blades is the trapezius. The trapezius' primary function is to raise the shoulder girdle. The latissimus dorsi (lats) are the large triangular muscles that extend from under the shoulders down to the small of the back on both sides. Their primary function is to pull the shoulders downward. The spinal erectors, composed of several muscles in the lower back that guard the nerve channels, work to hold the spine erect, straighten the spine from a position with torso flexed completely forward, and help to arch the lower and middle back.

4. Upper Back: Barbell Reverse Upright Row

I performed three sets increasing the weight 5-10 lbs each set. The first set I used a weight that allowed me to perform around 12 reps. The second set I performed 10 reps, and the third set I performed 6-8 reps. I stretched the muscles after each set using the back stretch.

1

begin

2

finish

3

stretch

DAY 5
ROUTINE

BACK,
BICEPS,
FOREARM,
ABS

5. Middle Back: Stiff Arm Pull-down

I performed three sets increasing the weight 5-10 lbs each set. The first set I used a weight that allowed me to perform around 12 reps. The second set I performed 10 reps, and the third set I performed 6-8 reps. I stretched the muscles after each set using the back stretch.

Note: A lower back exercise was performed on day 1 at the end of routine.

The Biceps

Biceps size and mass are important for defining a well developed biceps muscle; however, shape, definition and complete development are more important than pure size. The barbell curl had been the fundamental exercise I was using to develop my biceps. To develop the biceps further, I added movements that emphasized the length, thickness and height of the biceps. These varying exercises gave me a more complete quality of the muscle.

1. Mass of Biceps: Barbell Curl

I performed three sets increasing the weight 5-10 lbs each set. The first set I used a weight that allowed me to perform around 12 reps. The second set I performed 10 reps, and the third set I performed 6-8 reps. I stretched the muscles after each set using the biceps stretch.

DAY 5 ROUTINE

2. Length and Lower Thickness of Biceps: Incline Dumbbell Curl

I performed three sets increasing the weight 5-10 lbs each set. The first set I used a weight that allowed me to perform around 12 reps. The second set I performed 10 reps, and the third set I performed 6-8 reps. I stretched the muscles after each set using the biceps stretch.

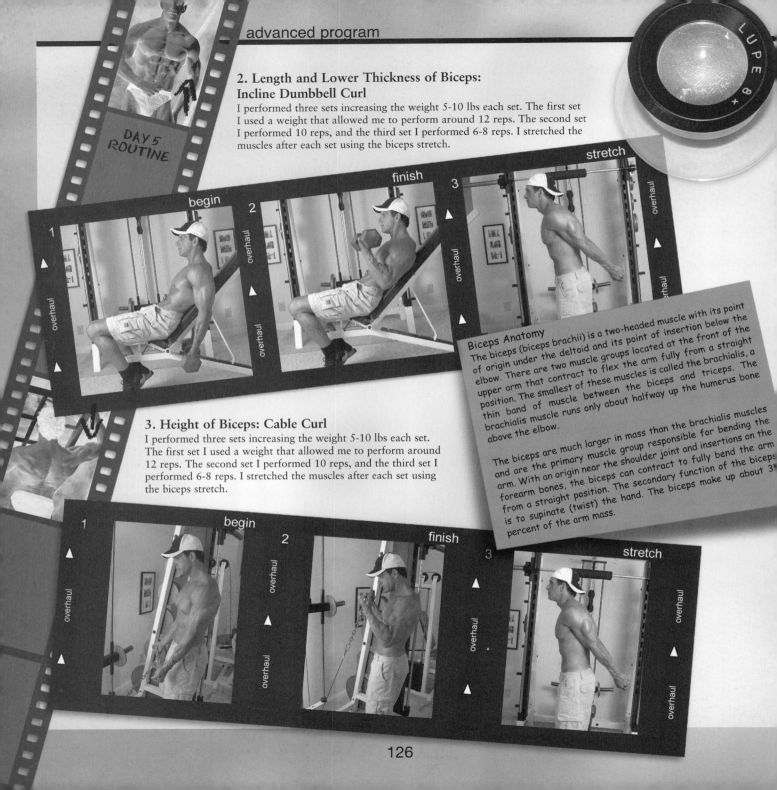

begin 1

finish 2

stretch 3

Biceps Anatomy

The biceps (biceps brachii) is a two-headed muscle with its point of origin under the deltoid and its point of insertion below the elbow. There are two muscle groups located at the front of the upper arm that contract to flex the arm fully from a straight position. The smallest of these muscles is called the brachialis, a thin band of muscle between the biceps and triceps. The brachialis muscle runs only about halfway up the humerus bone above the elbow.

The biceps are much larger in mass than the brachialis muscles and are the primary muscle group responsible for bending the arm. With an origin near the shoulder joint and insertions on the forearm bones, the biceps can contract to fully bend the arm from a straight position. The secondary function of the biceps is to supinate (twist) the hand. The biceps make up about 3" percent of the arm mass.

3. Height of Biceps: Cable Curl

I performed three sets increasing the weight 5-10 lbs each set. The first set I used a weight that allowed me to perform around 12 reps. The second set I performed 10 reps, and the third set I performed 6-8 reps. I stretched the muscles after each set using the biceps stretch.

begin 1

finish 2

stretch 3

DAY 5
ROUTINE

BACK,
BICEPS,
FOREARM,
ABS

4. Outside Biceps: Reverse Barbell Curl

I performed three sets increasing the weight 5-10 lbs each set. The first set
I used a weight that allowed me to perform around 12 reps. The second set
I performed 10 reps, and the third set I performed 6-8 reps. I stretched the
muscles after each set using the biceps stretch.

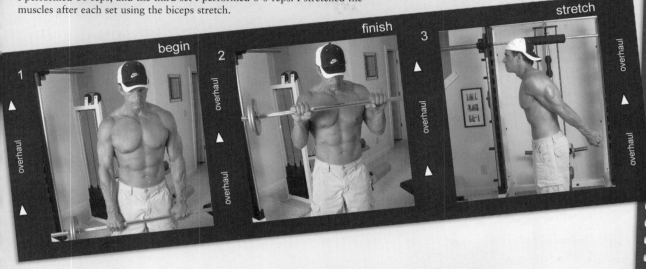

5. Inner Biceps: Wide Grip Barbell Curl

I performed three sets increasing the weight 5-10 lbs each set. The first set I used
a weight that allowed me to perform around 12 reps. The second set I performed
10 reps, and the third set I performed 6-8 reps. I stretched the muscles after each
set using the biceps stretch.

127

DAY 5 ROUTINE

1. Inner Forearms: Barbell Wrist Curl
I performed three sets increasing the weight 5-10 lbs each set.
I used a weight that allowed me to perform around 12-20 reps.

begin

1

finish

2

3

stretch

overhaul

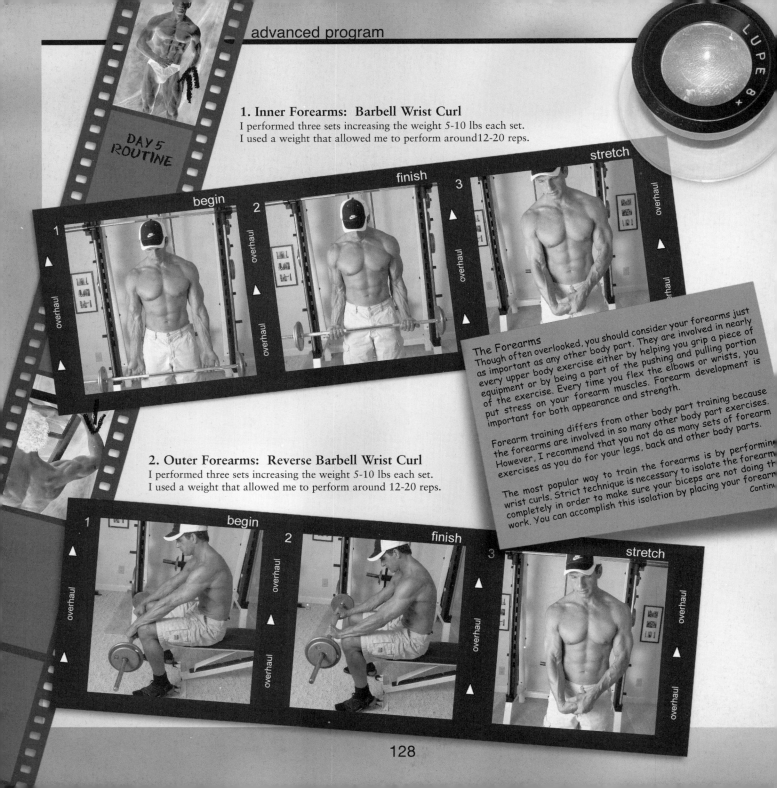

2. Outer Forearms: Reverse Barbell Wrist Curl
I performed three sets increasing the weight 5-10 lbs each set.
I used a weight that allowed me to perform around 12-20 reps.

begin

1

finish

2

3

stretch

overhaul

The Forearms

Though often overlooked, you should consider your forearms just as important as any other body part. They are involved in nearly every upper body exercise either by helping you grip a piece of equipment or by being a part of the pushing and pulling portion of the exercise. Every time you flex the elbows or wrists, you put stress on your forearm muscles. Forearm development is important for both appearance and strength.

Forearm training differs from other body part training because the forearms are involved in so many other body part exercises. However, I recommend that you not do as many sets of forearm exercises as you do for your legs, back and other body parts.

The most popular way to train the forearms is by performing wrist curls. Strict technique is necessary to isolate the forearm completely in order to make sure your biceps are not doing the work. You can accomplish this isolation by placing your forearm

Continu

DAY 5
ROUTINE

BACK,
BICEPS,
FOREARM,
ABS

THE ABDOMEN
1. Upper Abs: Crunch (Feet on Bench)
I performed three sets of 12-15 reps.

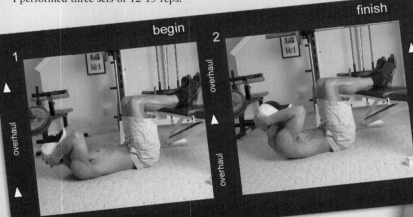

firmly on a bench with your elbows close together and locked in between your knees. If you try to do other upper body exercises when your wrists and forearms are fatigued you will severely limit your ability to train with intensity, so do your forearm exercises at the end of your workout.

Forearm Anatomy
The forearm is composed of a variety of muscles on the outside and inside of the lower arm that control the actions of the hand and wrist. The forearm flexor muscles curl the palm down and forward; the forearm extensor muscles curl the knuckles back and up.

2. Lower Abs: Hanging Leg Raise
I performed three sets of 12-15 reps.

DAY 5 ROUTINE

3. Intercostals: Incline Seated Twist
I performed three sets of 12-15 reps.

begin
1
2
3
finish
overhaul

4. Obliques: Seated Broomstick Twist
I performed one set of 100 reps.

begin
1
2
3
finish
overhaul

DAY 6 ROUTINE

Cardio day
Ride stationary Bike
for 30 minutes

DAY 7 START OVER

Too Much of a Good Thing

One of the reasons many people fail to get positive results from their programs is overtraining. Overtraining eventually results in frustration. It causes the person to think that he/she can't reach the goal, that he/she is a failure. These people feel like failures because they are trying as hard as they can but are not seeing positive results. In truth, however, they are not failures. They are merely failing to follow the program correctly.

Overtrainers still cling to the erroneous mindset that exercise means "no pain, no gain." That simply won't work. Training too much, too hard, too soon will not work. Part of the art of exercising is the ability to design your program so that it provides for sufficient training to induce physiological changes without exceeding your body's adaptive capabilities. Overtraining causes an imbalance between training and recovery. The symptoms of overtraining vary from individual to individual; however, some of the most common signs of overtraining are: impaired physical performance, reduced enthusiasm for training, increased resting heart rate, chronic muscle or joint soreness, nagging injuries, colds, flu, sickness, reduced appetite, weight loss, disturbed sleeping patterns, depression, irritability, anxiety or loss of sex drive.

When you are truly focused on your training, you are only aware of those things that are critical to your workout, to the exclusion of everything else.

What should you do if you suspect that you are overtraining? Take a break! Change your routine! Go on vacation!

Conclusion

If I'm training or working toward a specific goal, I might as well dig in and do as much quality work as I can while I'm there because if I prepare myself mentally to complete every task as efficiently as I can, with the highest quality of effort, I will meet my goals and still have time for myself, my family and my friends. By organizing your time, planning your workout, and setting specific daily goals, you can accomplish more while you are working out, have adequate rest time, and still have time left over for career, family, friends and fun.

When you are truly focused on your training, you are only aware of those things that are critical to your workout, to the exclusion of everything else. You and your training become one, and nothing else in the world exists during that time. Initially, focusing may feel like nonfocusing because you are allowing the routine to unfold automatically, free from directives or self evaluation. In the beginning stages, you may only be able to focus for short periods. That's fine. The more often you work at focusing, allowing it to become a natural part of everything you do, the easier it will become.

Focusing at this level is like allowing your body to function on automatic pilot. Your body leads the performance without any interference from negative distractions. When you are successfully focused, you will feel a connection between your body and what you are doing, just as the tennis pro feels as if his arm and hand are part of the racket. You will become aware of how your body feels when you execute a movement flawlessly.

Remember—your ultimate goal is to learn to read your body's signals and to let it dictate how much weight and how many times to lift. Be patient. It usually takes several years of training for someone to become intuitive to their body's training prescription.

PART 3

Challenge yourself and deal with uncertainty.
When you do so you become alive because uncertainty ignites passion!

The overriding justifier behind all action should be to improve one's self. You can't argue that everyone wants to look, feel, perform and live a healthy fulfilling life. All one's actions should be directed to support this better quality of life

Chapter 7

add the finishing touches

Before I overhauled my body and my life, I never paid more than $5 for a haircut. More often than not, I'd get a willing friend or family member to chop at my hair in the backyard. As long as I didn't have to think too much about it, what did I care? I didn't pay any attention to my clothes. I'd give it the sniff-test, and if it passed I'd wear it. To me the thought of shopping for clothes was torture, and I would have rather gone naked than ironed a pair of pants. And hair and skin products? Forget it. I was a football player. I used the deodorant soap in the locker room on my body and my hair.

All that was fine for my college days, but when I was out in the real world struggling paycheck to paycheck, I still had those bad habits. Then I was worrying about putting food on the table—moisturizing my scalp was pretty low on my to-do list. I was in such a fog just trying to get by that I didn't notice how I looked. It never occurred to me that every day I was presenting myself poorly to other people.

As I worked through my own overhaul, I began to become more aware of my overall appearance. When I stepped into the business world, I was suddenly in a white-collar situation where dress and image were very important. I started to watch the top executives in all types of business. It was obvious those CEOs knew that how they presented themselves made a huge difference. Their image was important for the image of the company.

Way back all those years ago when I had sketched that image of the "ultimate me," that person had it all together. I knew that to come closer to making that image a reality, I needed to add these finishing touches.

My first steps were simple ones. I stopped wearing all the old baggy clothes that I had worn when I was overweight, and I started wearing clothes that fit me. Wearing clothes that fit me was a step out of my comfort zone. I had often hidden my body under those big clothes. It felt odd to buy a medium T-shirt instead of an XXL—it felt even odder to wear it! I discovered that I didn't have to buy expensive clothes in order to look good. Now that my body was in shape, even inexpensive clothes fit better.

It is an investment in your self-confidence— and who knows where that could lead you?

I began to develop my own personal style. I didn't spend hours at the mall or subscribe to fashion magazines, I just started to take more pride in my appearance. I urge you not to overlook your wardrobe. Don't wear your old "fat clothes" simply because they're comfortable. You've worked hard at reshaping your body, now wear clothes that flatter you. Wearing those big clothes, especially if you've lost a lot of weight, only makes you look sickly. Spend a little money and update your clothing. It is an investment in your self-confidence—and who knows where that could lead you?

It was about this time that I met Angela. She was a young star in the salon business, and I was a guy who used to use bar soap to wash his hair. Every day she helped people remake their images. People came to her feeling down about themselves, but when they left her, they looked and felt great. I knew she was talented and that I could trust her, so I took the next step.

As I've said, I rarely put any time or money into my hair and skin, so the salon was a fish-out-of-water experience for me in the beginning. I know many men feel the same way. "That's woman territory. I'll stick with my barber and his clippers, thank you very much." But Angela created a great cut for me, easily the best I'd ever had. Because it worked with my naturally coarse and curly hair, it was easy to take care of and it looked good. Because of her years of experience, she could spot my skin problems, she knew what I could do to help my thinning hair. I began to realize that the stuff we men are afraid of can really help! Both men and women need to realize a great cut and the right hair and skin products can do so much for your appearance.

Just as with the new clothes, taking care of my skin and hair was another step out of my comfort zone. I felt strange at first, but when I saw the affect on my appearance and my self-confidence, I was glad I had risked feeling uncomfortable. It was another small, easy change that I could make to improve my daily life.

As a young man, I would have laughed at the thought of me in the beauty business, but here I am. Angela and I own a salon, and I spend my life helping people be their best in all aspects—from their career to their body to how they look. Even though I wouldn't have guessed it back then, now it is the most satisfying thing I can imagine.

I've never felt like I was showing someone how to work out; I felt like I was showing them how to better themselves and improve the quality of their life.

It all goes back to the image of the ultimate you. Once you start to change your life, the easier change becomes. As the momentum builds toward improving yourself, you become more aware. Each step brought me closer to that image. It's like walking into a room with a pair of dirty socks on the floor. If the whole room is in a mess, you barely notice the socks. But if the rest of the room is neat and orderly when you walk in, the socks on the floor stand out. Thats how it was with my hair and clothing. Back when I was down and out, I wouldn't have had the courage to change my wardrobe or take care of my skin. I never would have thought about it if I hadn't rebuilt myself. But with my overhaul, it was like icing on the cake. I wanted to do it. I wanted to keep improving myself. I wanted to be my personal best.

It's about presenting the best you that you can to the world.

Some people consider paying attention to the details of your appearance to be vain or trivial. I do not. I would never judge people for ignoring these details, because I've been there too. But you can be sure that rock stars and professional athletes and business moguls pay attention to these details. If it boosts your confidence and helps you accomplish your goals, why not? The whole point isn't having just the right clothes or the trendiest hairstyle, it's about marketing yourself. It's about presenting the best you that you can to the world. If you truly feel you are the best you can be without any work on this aspect of your appearance, then terrific. But if you need a little help in this area so you can be at your peak, keep reading. In the next chapter Angela shares her expertise with you, just like she did with me. You've come this far, why not add those finishing touches and fulfill the dream of the ultimate you?

Chapter 8

putting on the polish

Editor's note: In this chapter Angela trades her scissors for a keyboard to write about her many years of experience with personal style makeovers.

Everyone can look good. I believe that. Not everyone is a classic beauty, and it would be boring if everyone were. But everyone can work with what they were given and look good. What many people fail to understand is that looking good is a choice, not some magical gift. You have to be willing to put in the time and effort to look your best. But don't worry, it doesn't have to consume your whole life and, even though beauty is a billion dollar industry, it doesn't have to be so confusing. That's why I'm here. Let me give you the basics so you can begin to finish your overhaul and define your own personal style.

I have been in the salon industry for over 20 years, and I've owned my own salon for 12 years. I have such a passion for what I do that it's hard to believe I almost chose a different career. I went to college to become a nurse, but I was more and more attracted to the beauty industry. Hair and makeup was something I had always enjoyed. So I decided to take the plunge. I dropped out of college and signed up for beauty school. I waited tables at night to pay for my classes, and I lived with my sister while she attended college. I have never regretted my choice. My goal was to own my own salon by the time I was 30— a goal I achieved. I have reached the status where I can pick and chose my clientele, work hours that allow for personal and family time, and people come from other states for appointments in my salon. And best of all, even after 20 years, I still think my job is so much fun! I love the instant gratification of making someone look their best.

I have learned a lot about helping people look their best during my years in the beauty industry. In fact, I even have my own line of hair care products called ANGELA HAIR NUTRIENTS™. Here are a few of the things that I feel are the most important in taking care of the finishing touches that complete a successful overhaul.

> When it comes to hair, getting and maintaining a good cut is the most important thing you can do.

Great Hair

When it comes to hair, getting and maintaining a good cut is the most important thing you can do. If you have a good cut, your hair's going to lay better no matter what you do. It sounds like a cliché, but when you look good, you feel good. You have different outfits, but you wear your hair every single day. Having a great hairstyle helps with the cycle of treating yourself well. You feel better about yourself; it makes you do your job better; it makes you a better wife, husband, mother, father, friend. You just like yourself better.

But how do you get a good cut? Well, finding the right stylist is important. Ask around—word of mouth is usually the best way to find a good stylist. A stylist's work speaks for its self, so ask people who have great hair. Avoid a rash walk-in appointment and always schedule a consultation. Your stylist must not only have the technical skills needed, but also the communication skills.

A good stylist will take the time to listen to what you want and will ask questions about your lifestyle. How much time do you have to spend on your hair? What image do you want to project? Will the cut you want work with the natural texture of your hair? Will the shape of your face be flattered by the cut you want? Pictures of hairstyles you like are very helpful, but be flexible. The style you like may not always be a style that will work well for your day-to-day life. Living with a hairstyle is a lot like living with a fitness plan—make sure it fits your life. If you try to change your life to fit a hairstyle (or fitness plan) it will end up a failure. Listen to your stylist and take their advice. They are professionals, and if they've taken the time to listen to you they will know what will work for you and what won't.

The same thing goes for color. Good color is so much more than a box from the drugstore. A professional colorist will know what colors will work with your skin tone. They will give you advice about keeping your color and the effect of the water in your area on your color. Find a stylist who listens to you—then listen to him!

Once you've found a stylist who can give you a cut that fits you, the next step is a basic hair care regimen. Get a trim every six to eight weeks and use high-quality salon products: shampoo, daily conditioner and a weekly deep conditioning treatment. I've found it best to choose salon products and remain brand loyal. Pass on the cheaper shampoos and conditioners you can buy at the grocery store. If you don't want to take my word on it, prove it to yourself. Try the salon-quality products for six weeks. You will see and feel the difference in your hair. The cheaper shampoos and conditioners leave build-up on your scalp, they don't nourish your hair, and you spend more in the long run because you have to use more of the product.

> ## Basic Hair Care Regimen
>
> -Regular trim-ups
>
> -Salon-quality Shampoo
>
> -Salon-quality daily conditioner
>
> -Salon-quality weekly deep conditioning treatment

Cremes and pomades and extra products aren't necessary for healthy hair, but they might be necessary to keep the style you want. Often people complain they can't duplicate the look their stylist creates. It is important to use the products the stylist uses in creating the look you love.

Skin Care and Makeup

Another very important aspect of caring for your appearance is skin care. And just as with your hair, you need a basic skin care regimen. It's best to start taking care of your skin before you develop wrinkles and spots, but don't despair if you haven't been doing it and you notice your skin doesn't look so good. No matter when you start, you will see improvement in your skin.

Good color is so much more than a box from the drugstore.

The basic skin care regimen for men and women includes cleanser, toner, moisturizer, and sunscreen. Sunscreen can be combined with another step: moisturizer or, for women, makeup. Many of those products include sunscreen. It is my belief that skipping the sun protection is the biggest mistake people make with their skin—especially men. Many doctors and skin specialists believe you should have absolutely no tan. I don't go that far. I like to have a little color, but be sensible about it.

While men are becoming more and more willing to follow a good hair care regimen, I find they still reject good skin care. They think nothing of getting a sunburn, and they don't want to be caught using "girlie" products. There are more and more quality skin lines being marketed to men, and men are beginning to realize how beneficial those products can be. A few years ago, most men would never have used hair gel, but now it isn't a big deal. I believe it will be the same way with men's skin care.

Choosing the right products for your skin care regimen can be a daunting task. There are so many products out there, and what works for a friend's skin may not work for yours. I recommend professional advice. Depending on your budget, make an appointment with a dermatologist, a spa, or with a department store consultant or a representative for a home sales makeup line. When you seek out advice, look at that person's skin. Does it look good? There is no point in wasting your time and money on products they recommend if their own skin looks bad.

I recommend at least an annual appointment at a day spa. It can be difficult to find the time, but I find it is worth it. A good professional facial cleans away all the old skin and the estheticians keep me abreast of changes in my skin. Age and events such as pregnancy or menopause change your skin and what it needs. It can be hard to know how to deal with those changes, but that is what they specialize in.

Like with hair products, I do recommend brand loyalty in your skin care program. Often the products are designed to work together. For the best results stick with the same brand of cleanser, toner and moisturizer. And when you switch to a new skin care line or begin a regimen, give your skin time to adapt to the change. It can take your skin a week or two to get used to a product change. At first your skin might actually look worse, but be patient. Stick with the regime and you will see and feel results.

As I mentioned earlier, too much sun exposure is the biggest mistake people make with their skin, but it isn't the only one. I often see two other mistakes: not cleansing daily and not getting proper nutrition. It is important to cleanse your face at least once a day—twice is best. Ladies, don't go to bed with your makeup on no matter how tired you are. Good nutrition, especially drinking plenty of water, helps both your skin and your hair. If you eat a lot of junky food and

The basic skin care regimen for men and women includes cleanser, toner, moisturizer, and sunscreen.

drink a lot of alcohol, it shows in your skin and hair. Nutrition is so important. Good nutrition gives you more energy, a sharper mind, and a better appearance! It's a no-brainer. Eat right.

Good nutrition, especially drinking plenty of water, helps both your skin and your hair.

The Most Common Skin Care Mistakes
1. Too much sun exposure
2. Not cleansing daily
3. Poor nutrition/not drinking enough water

While good skin care is foundational, makeup is a great extra that can help define a woman's style. Besides, ladies, let's admit it, it's fun! It makes us feel good. We can be natural or glamorous or fresh-faced or mysterious simply by choosing different types of makeup. Unlike hair and skin products where I recommend getting the highest-quality products you can afford, there is a lot more wiggle room when it comes to makeup. If you find you like expensive brands and you can swing it, then I say splurge! If you don't want to spend that much, you will probably be just as happy using what you can buy at the drugstore. The only caveat is if you have sensitive skin, you may find some cheaper brands irritate you. I have very sensitive eyes and there are some brands of mascara and eyeshadow that are uncomfortable for me to wear. There's no way to know what brands won't work for you, but if you tend to have skin allergies opt for hypoallergenic cosmetics.

When buying makeup you do need to avoid getting in a rut. We all know people who wear the same makeup all the time, night or day, for years and years. The thing happens with hairstyles. You become used to what you see every morning in the mirror and you stop evaluating that look. That's why you see women wearing the same beehive they had in the 60s or the thick, black eyeliner they wore in the 80s. Have a professional update your makeup occasionally or experiment with new colors.

When you change your makeup or your hairstyle make a commitment to yourself to keep the updated look for at least two weeks. Give yourself a chance to get used to the look and to learn how to easily recreate it each morning. We've all had a hairstyle that we thought looked great when we left the salon, but that we had given up on 10 days later. It feels easier to style it the old way, it takes less time and it feels more comfortable. We let ourselves slip back to the old look we wanted to change in the first place! Give yourself a chance to feel comfortable with new hairstyles and new makeup. If after two-three weeks you still don't like it, then you've given yourself a chance and you can try something else.

Cosmetic Surgery

When you cut hair for a living, people will sit down in your chair and tell you all sorts of things. And cosmetic surgery is no exception. I've had many, many clients have all sorts of work done. Most have been happy with the results; others, not so much. Kris and I have clients ask us for advice and recommendations based on what we hear from clients. I'm no doctor, but I know what the dish is on plastic surgery. Don't think of what I write here as a professional consultation; think of it as really good girl talk. It isn't for everyone, and I'm not saying you have to have work done to look good. But it's certainly not something you should feel ashamed of, either.

Good nutrition gives you more energy, a sharper mind, and a better appearance!

145

First of all, some people are good candidates for plastic surgery, some people are bad candidates. A bad candidate has unrealistic expectations of what surgery will do for him or her. They expect miracles. They don't want to eat right or exercise; they want liposuction to make them look like model. That won't work. They still have all the bad habits that got them there in the first place. Or someone who thinks their big nose is keeping them from being happy. They will be the same person after the surgery. A new nose won't really fix what is truly wrong in their life.

> You become used to what you see every morning in the mirror and you stop evaluating that look.

A good candidate is someone who is basically confident and happy with themselves. They don't believe they need to have plastic surgery, but they want it. I had one client who was in great shape, but she wasn't happy with her butt. She was considering liposuction, but she said, "I'm giving it a full year of eating healthy and exercising four or five times a week. If that doesn't take care of my butt, I'm doing it." She was doing everything right. She had good habits and she wasn't relying on a magic surgery to turn her life around. She wasn't doing it to please somebody else, she wanted it for herself.

If you think cosmetic surgery is for you, you owe it to yourself to find the best plastic surgeon you can. You will be paying this doctor a lot of money to permanently alter your appearance. Make sure he knows what he's doing. Ask around, find which surgeons others would (and wouldn't) recommend. Many people who have had work done don't advertise it, but most are willing to talk candidly about their experience when asked.

After getting some word-of-mouth references, schedule consultations with at least three different surgeons. Educate yourself about the procedure you are interested in and ask questions. Make sure the doctor specializes in the procedure you want done. That means when you want a boob job, don't go to a doctor who specializes in nose jobs. Steer clear of doctors who claim to do it all. My experience has been a doctor who focuses on one or two types of procedures is a better way to go. Also, by finding someone who specializes in the procedure you want and by asking questions, you can avoid being some doctor's guinea pig. Unfortunately, doctors can attend weekend conferences to learn some cosmetic procedures and be performing them in their office on Monday.

That means when you want a boob job, don't go to a doctor who specializes in nose jobs.

If after consulting with physicians you are ready to have a procedure done, I recommend not telling everyone about it. Hopefully it will look so natural afterward that people won't be able to put their finger on what's different about you. It's better to hear, "Oh, you look great!" than, "Oh, you've had your eyes done!" Plastic surgery does carry a stigma with some people, and it may be easier for you just to avoid their judgments by being discreet. Of course, if you are a very open person and you have no qualms about what others know about your personal life, feel free to tell everyone you know!

Most of the people I know who have had plastic surgery have been very happy with the results. Rhinoplasty, breast augmentation, face lifts, whatever—most of my clients say they would do it again in a heartbeat. They have loved the results. Even clients who experienced challenges such as infections or painful recovery periods were still pleased with the final results. I have, however, heard clients who've had liposuction say that if they could do it over again, they wouldn't. It can be quite painful and the look and feel of the body isn't always what was expected.

Ultimately its your attitude that will light the shadows on your face.

I myself have had breast augmentation and some facial work done—and I love the results. I am so happy I chose to do it. I always had a large lump on the bridge of my nose. It was kind of a trademark for me. I felt like I looked good before my nose job, and Kris didn't really want me to have it done. But it was something I wanted to do for me. I'm thrilled with my new nose.

After having children, I wasn't happy with the change in my breasts. No amount of exercise was going to bring them back. So I decided to have a boob job. Unlike my nose job, Kris was all for this one! Whether I look sexier now isn't really the issue—I feel sexier! I feel sexy and confident, and it shows. Implants have been controversial in the past, but I have no regrets. They are proportionate to my body, and they look and feel great.

Be Your Best

You should not feel ashamed about wanting to look your best. Don't worry about what others will think of you. Remember, people who truly want to see you succeed and live a life that you are excited about will support your efforts. When you take care of yourself, it shows that you are of value. Like the commercial says, "I'm worth it." I'm not advocating spending hours and hours in front of the mirror, but I am saying that when you look good, you feel great. When you feel great, you will do great things. Your life's goal shouldn't be to look good, but looking good can help you achieve your life's goals. And that's what *Overhaul* is all about!

Chapter 9

expose yourself

You have all that you need to make serious change a reality in your life. You have the power to become a superstar. But do you still feel a little fear about risking the comfort of the status quo? Let me tell you a story that might help you get past that fear.

Angela and I had only been married about a year when one day she called me as I was working in my office. A local AIDS hospice was preparing for their annual fundraising campaign, and an acquaintance had asked Angela if I would be willing to pose for their poster. The photographer would use the photos and poster all year to promote fundraising and the campaign would kick-off with a black-tie gala. It's a big deal in the community, especially the beauty industry.

"You've got to do it," said Angela. "You won't get paid, but it's for charity. They just want to use your chest. Your face and the rest of your body won't be in the picture."

I thought, sure, I can donate my time. I've had my body parts featured in plenty of ads. Why not? Piece of cake. So I agreed.

On the day of the photo shoot, I walked into the studio and met the photographer and his staff. While they prepared their equipment I sat on a couch and waited next to a blonde woman wearing a skin-colored body suit. She introduced herself and asked if I was there for the photo shoot. I said yes, and she said, "Me, too. I'm going to be in it with you."

Hm. In the photo with me? That was the first clue that things were not going to be what I had expected.

The photographer's assistant walked over and announced they were almost ready. He showed me to a dressing room where he said I could get ready. "There's not much to get ready," I thought to myself. "I'm just taking off my shirt." I had been painting my house that day, and I had planned on the photo shoot taking less than an hour. I was still even wearing my paint-spattered work clothes. But I've worked many photo shoots, and I'm not shy in front of the camera. So I took off my shirt and headed for the set.

The female model was already on the set, wearing a wig of blonde, curly hair that fell past her thighs. The assistant had positioned her cowboy-style on a chair—she sat on the seat backward with her legs straddling the back of the chair. She had her arms folded over the back of the chair, and the long hair from the wig tumbled around her.

As I walked out, I looked at the photographer. He and several others were looking at a camera, and I could see from his frustrated look, that there was a problem with it. He looked up and saw me and said, "Kris, go ahead and sit on the floor in front her. We've got to mess with this camera, but we'll be right back."

So I did as I was asked to do, I sat on the floor in front of her in the chair. I sat facing the camera, with my back to the model. "I wonder what's wrong with the camera?" I asked, idling making small talk with her. I turned my head around to look at her as I spoke, and when I did, there I was, eye-level with—well, let's just say, remember that skin-colored body-suit? It was gone. She was completely naked!

I snapped my head back around. She responded to my question, but I had no idea what she said. I was too busy thinking, "Stay calm. Stay calm." Inside I was freaking out wondering what was going on, but on the outside I was trying to act all cool about the fact that a gorgeous blonde model was unexpectedly nude right behind me.

About then the photographer returned to begin taking photos. After a couple shots, he looked around from behind the camera and said, "Kris, those pants aren't going to work." OK. Not a problem. I'm a professional. I have on posing trunks under my pants, they're like binikis. I'm too embarrassed and still a little too stunned to ask just what is going on here. All I can think about is getting this over with so I can get the hell out of here. I mean, really, how many chest photos can they take?

Then I realize that the photographer isn't even taking photos of my chest. The shot is too wide. It is obvious that all of me—from my head to my toes-is in this shot. And now the photographer is saying the tiny trunks I'm wearing are a problem! What?!

I finally find my bearings. "What are we doing here?" I asked. They explain the image they are after. The model and I are supposed to look naked, but with nothing actually showing. I'm supposed to be cutting her long hair with a pair of giant scissors. The slogan is, "Cut off AIDS."

The truth is I'm uncomfortable, but I kept telling myself it was for a good cause. Just get it over with. "So how do you do a shot like this?" I asked. "Get rid of the underwear, and we'll tape you," he answered. "Tape me" apparently meant taping a tiny paper napkin between my legs and up my back side.

Now I'm really embarrassed. I'm next to a nude woman. There's a room full of people looking at me. I look like I'm wearing a diaper. It's hot under the lights, I'm nervous and I begin to sweat. The tape won't hold to my perspiring skin, and my little napkin starts to fall off. This is not what I had in mind when I was volunteered.

For the next pose the photographer places the model on top of me! She's naked straddling my leg. The tape? It's long gone. I'm trying to be professional, but in my head I'm thinking, "This has turned into a porno! What do I do?" Guys, you think being naked with a beautiful model is a dream come true? Let me tell you, it ain't. It's mortifying. The only blood going anywhere is to your face as it turns beet red.

The model and I are posed in what I can only describe as a simulated sex act when the photographer yells, "Don't move!" The camera has locked up and they are changing equipment. We're standing there naked, and I'm trying to think of something to say. "Aren't you kind of embarrassed with all of these guys in the room looking at you?" I asked. She laughed, "Honey, they aren't looking at me. They're looking at you."

"Huh?" I asked. I didn't understand.

"I know all these guys," she said. "They're all gay."

That scenario hadn't occurred to me. Now I was really self-conscious. This situation just kept getting more and more embarrassing. I wanted to leave, but I knew walking out would cost a lot of money in studio time and photographer fees. Besides, it couldn't get any worse. Could it?

That's when I saw the film crew. They were filming a documentary that would be shown at the gala to kick off the fundraising campaign. The most important people in the city would be at that dinner. Not to mention everyone in the salon industry—people that Angela and I know and work with! And I was standing there naked with a nude stranger wrapped around me!

At that point I felt as though all the air in me had been sucked from my lungs. This was too humiliating. What was I going to do?

When I got home and told Angela what had happened, she was livid. She had encouraged me to do the shoot because she had been misled. When I saw the final version of the poster, I was stunned. The model was on her knees in front of me. I was looking down at her cutting her hair with the giant scissors. We were both facing the camera, but with all the hair from the wig over her face, it looked like she was facing me. It was obvious we were naked, and it looked like she was giving me—well, I think you get the picture. They made postcards of the poster, printed thousands of them and put them on sale as a fundraiser in every salon in the city. Everyone that Angela and I knew in the salon industry had not only seen the photos, they also had their very own copies!

Do you want to know what shocked me the most about that whole awful experience? The world kept turning. What I mean is, it doesn't get much worse than that. Yet, my fear of what people would think was actually much worse than how they really reacted. Surprisingly, many people even treated me with more respect. Besides, how they reacted didn't bother me as much as I thought it would. I found strength in that humiliation. That episode elevated me to a level that helped me become a more successful person. It freed me from a lot of insecurities—it was like removing shackles. I'm freer to take risks now. What if my business fails? What if my book doesn't sell? What if I mess up during a speaking engagement in front of important people? So what—I'll survive. I've been in one of the most embarrassing situations imaginable and my world didn't come apart. I can risk a little embarrassment for the chance of greater success. The fear of looking stupid doesn't hold me back.

It's a good example of what I'm trying to teach in this book. Don't hold yourself back out of fear or to try to please others. Peel away the facade of who you think others think you should be and expose the real you. The world will react positively to the real you. That's when success comes. Take the risk and dare to live the life you have always dreamed. Go ahead—expose yourself!

Chapter 10

getting from resolution to reality

As you finish reading this book, I want you to think about the questions I asked you back in the first chapter: Are you the person you want to be? Are you living the life you wish you could? Do you always look and feel your best? Do you always perform at your peak? If not, why? What's holding you back? Your weight? Your appearance? Your lack of confidence?

Let's think a little deeper. Don't we go to the salon, lift weights, run the mile and skip desert all in an effort to look, feel and perform the best we can? Isn't all this fuss really an attempt to connect to our true self—the person we truly want to be deep down inside?

My goal in writing this book was to give you a tool to help you find the place where happiness, success and fulfillment lie—within your true self. *Overhaul* is, at its core, about connecting to your true self. Hopefully after reading this book you have discovered that unveiling yourself is important in the quest for a happy life. When you settle for what you are instead of what you can be, you'll live in a constant state of anxiety because what you are is not what you want to be. Living that way produces conflict, and conflict produces anxiety. Happiness can't be found in an anxious state!

As I continue to travel the world promoting the Overhaul concept, I see so many people who live each and every day in this anxious state. They are overweight, out of shape, unhappy, unfulfilled, depressed, helpless. I hope that in *Overhaul* I

I consider a successful Overhaul as reaching the point where you feel good about yourself.

have shown you that it doesn't have to be that way. I have provided you with a life-changing formula, so you can be one of the lucky ones who experiences life as a fit, energetic, healthy, happy, confident person.

I consider a successful overhaul as reaching the point where you feel good about yourself. When you feel good about yourself, you project your own greatness and the rest of the world feeds on it and responds positively to you. In this state you will be more successful in your career, relationships and endeavors. But this exciting, magical state can only exist when you take charge and work to continually improve and better yourself. It may seem strange at first. In fact the idea of overhauling your appearance and using it as a self-development tool stymies even successful people.

Living true to who you are is where success and happiness are found. They aren't found in trying to please others. When you live for the approval of others you live by their limits. Personal greatness can't be found there! When you worry about the opinions of other people, you can't focus on developing your own potential. You become "outer-directed" instead of "inner-inspired." Greatness can only be discovered when you are willing to strip down and expose your true self. Most people harbor who they really want to be opting to hold themselves back because of what they think others want for them. We let their opinions hold us back from clearly expressing our true desires to the world. And consequently we prevent ourselves from being who we want to be and achieving the life we secretly desire. How we frame our desires and how we define the benefits we expect from those desires will determine what drives us forward and how far it will take us. All motivations arise from the desire to be satisfied with yourself. But keep in mind that although desire is a key prerequisite for change, to get from resolution to reality requires a great deal of focus, dedication and persistence.

The basic fundamentals outlined in this book are important to understand and apply. They are the seeds of change. Results will come from the consistent application of basic fundamentals. These fundamentals will be the foundation of your success.

When you feel good about yourself, you project your own greatness and the rest of the world feeds on it and responds positively to you.

The secret to you changing your life is changing your thoughts. Thoughts control your life. They control what you become. Learn to leave your old thoughts and perceptions about yourself behind you. The way you think about yourself from now on will control your body, your appearance and your destiny. Your ability to develop a mental image of the ultimate you will be crucial to your success. This new way of thinking about yourself is where inspiration, motivation, direction and action will come from.

Beware! Your current situation—the one that you are unhappy with and wish to improve—still offers a sense of comfort and familiarity. Although you want to change your situation, in a strange sense it provides a sense of security. It feels like home, and even though you are unhappy there, you might find yourself tempted to hang around. Let me warn you. To stay there means stagnation, a lack of movement. If you can't move ahead you're not growing. Instead you're dying physically, emotionally, and you will live life unfulfilled. The only way to grow and move forward is to push yourself out of your comfort zone and take risks. CHALLENGE YOURSELF AND DEAL WITH UNCERTAINTY. WHEN YOU DO SO, YOU BECOME ALIVE BECAUSE UNCERTAINTY IGNITES PASSION!

The way you think about yourself from now on will control your body, your appearance and your destiny.

For the last 20 years I have been developing and testing the principles of this book. I have dedicated myself to discovering these secrets and implementing them into my life. They have not only transformed me physically, but have reinvented my life, giving it meaning and direction and awarding me much success. I have been able to see these principles reinvent, rebuild and remake others. Their lives have been transformed. Through this book, I have shared them with you. Now use them! Strip down and expose your true self! Become the star you were born to be!

Angela
Hair Nutrients.

O
V
E
R
H
A
U
L

www.trainingyourself.com

Kris Gebhardt and his wife, Angela, have decades of experience in fitness and beauty and own multiple businesses within the industries. With his chiseled physique and Angela's cover-girl beauty, they are the model couple for the fitness and beauty industries.

Combining their unique experience and expertise—beauty meets fitness—the couple have developed Angela Hair Nutrients, their own product line of nutrient-based hair and skin care products. They own the upscale Angela Salons and Gebhardt Consulting Inc. consulting entrepreneurs, individuals and corporations helping them design fitness and hair salon facilities.

Kris has written five books, including *Training Yourself*, *Body Mastery* and *Training the Teenager for the Game of Their Life*. Through his books and seminars he has dedicated his life to teaching others about the true value of

ABOUT THE AUTHOR

fitness and sharing his unique philosophy of using fitness as a self-development tool—showing how one cannot only use fitness to improve health but also the quality of one's life.

The couple have been featured in numerous publications and are frequent TV and radio guests. Kris has been officially recognized by Senator Richard Lugar and named one of the "Top 40 Under 40" business performers for 2003 by IBJ Magazine. He has coached many high-profile clients including rock stars, supermodels and Fortune 500 CEOs. He has also consulted and trained the cast of the Tony and Emmy Award-winning Broadway show, *Blast!*

The couple live in Indianapolis with their four children.

CONTRIBUTORS

18" Sculpture of Dejah Thoris and Tars Tarkas from the book *John Carter of Mars*. Sculpted in 2003.

Heather Lowhorn

Heather Lowhorn has worked as a writer and an editor for the past nine years. She has edited over 100 books, written dozens of magazine articles and, of course, worked on the countless boring business brochures and reports that freelancers have to endure to earn a living. She lives in Pendleton, Indiana, with her husband, their two children and a smelly old dog named Toby. "Having small children means diaper changes and peanut butter and jelly sandwiches take up most of my energy, but writing gives me the chance to learn new things and meet interesting people while allowing me the freedom to enjoy time with my family," she says. "On the down side, my dog sleeps under my desk. He really stinks. I'm thinking of changing his food."

Phil Velikan

Phil Velikan has been a free-range graphic/production artist for 10 years and has designed every sort of printed material you can imagine. He has produced over 200 book covers, and along with creating interior illustrations, he teaches Photoshop, all while running his company VIG in the confines of a hidden underground base in Brownsburg, Indiana. He currently has a wife and one and three quarters legal clones, a mutant cat and a yard full of moles. He is an accomplished woodworker and in his spare time does a bit of painting and sculpting. Hire him. He can be reached at pvelikan@indy.rr.com.

Heather Lowhorn hard at work editing this book.

HILL|PHOTOGRAPHY

www.trainingyourself.com